C000286114

OXYGEN FOR THE SOUL

*Prayers, Reflections and
Inspiration for Teenagers*

VERITAS

Published 2015 by
Veritas Publications
7–8 Lower Abbey Street
Dublin 1, Ireland

publications@veritas.ie
www.veritas.ie

ISBN 978-1-84730-663-0

10 9 8 7 6 5 4 3 2 1

A catalogue record for this book is available from the
British Library.

Designed by Lir Mac Cárthaigh
Printed in the Republic of Ireland by Colour World Print
Ltd, Kilkenny

*Veritas books are printed on paper made from the wood
pulp of managed forests. For every tree felled, at least
one tree is planted, thereby renewing natural resources.*

CONTENTS

FOR ELAINE

*With special thanks to the staff and students of
Loreto College, St Stephen's Green, Dublin*

INTRODUCTION

Prayer is the Oxygen of the Soul
ST PADRE PIO

Prayer is about being attentive to the presence of God in our lives. Martin Luther King, Jr said, 'To be a Christian without prayer is no more possible than to be alive without breathing.' Through prayer we can breathe life into our relationship with God by expressing our needs and hopes, our anger and frustrations, our sadness and joy. This book contains traditional prayers that are well known, as well as contemporary prayers and reflections. The authors vary from saints to secondary school students. Within this book you will hopefully find some words to help you begin your conversation with God.

ALWAYS PRAY, PRAY ALL WAYS

Pray through your Photos

Use photographs as an opportunity to thank God for the precious people in your life. Scroll through your photographs and whatever one you land on pray with gratitude for that memory, the good times you have had, the places you have been and the people you love.

Pray over your Food

Take a moment to be thankful for the food you are about to eat and be aware of where it has come from. Say a prayer of thanks for all who have worked so you have food to eat.

Pray on the Move

While making your way to school, look around at people going about their business. Choose one person and offer a prayer for them and their day.

Pray while Brushing your Teeth

In the morning, pray that today your smile will brighten someone's day, and at night say a prayer of thanks for all the things that made you smile throughout the day.

Pray to your Favourite Song

God loves music – it is found throughout the Bible. As St Augustine said, 'To sing is to pray twice'. Songs, whether they are happy or sad, can help us communicate with God. Listening to lyrics, dancing to our favourite song or singing can all be a form of prayer.

Pray Holding your Pet

God loves animals even more than we do. In fact, our relationship with them in many ways mirrors our relationship with God. If you have a pet that loves you unconditionally, let this love remind you of God's unconditional love for you.

Pray in Nature

Creation is a window into God's heart. In the woods, by the sea, beside a lake or in a garden we find aspects of God's nature reflected in visible ways. Spend some time noticing the incredible beauty and detail of creation. Remember that God also created you, and you are incredible and beautiful in God's eyes.

Pray Gazing at the Stars

Looking up at the sky on a starry night can remind us of how small we are in a vast universe. And yet, as we look to the night sky, the twinkling stars can remind us that God watches over us, being our light in the darkness and guiding us on each step of our journey.

Pray with the News

Whether you read or watch the news, or just follow what is trending on Twitter, being aware of what is going on in the world can put our own lives into perspective. Rather than feeling helpless about the problems in the world, it is good to remember that God cares about the world, and we can make a difference by praying for people. We can also pray for those who work to make the world a better place and reflect on how we can make a difference.

Pray while Exercising

Use the rhythm of exercise to create prayer routines and patterns. With every other step on a walk, for instance, name someone you want to pray for, or a gift you are thankful for, or a fear you need to overcome.

Pray in Silence and in Stillness

The Bible says, 'Be still and know that I am God.' Our days are filled with rushed activity and noise. Finding a few moments to sit still in silence can be a powerful prayer. Take some time out to be still and allow your thoughts to move towards God.

Pray through Written Words

Keeping a prayer journal can be a really helpful way to pray. Let your words and thoughts tumble onto a page and imagine God responding to you with a loving message of hope.

Pray through Art

God is the creator and we are made in the image of God so we all have the ability to be creative. Spending some time drawing, colouring or doodling can help relax our minds and can be the perfect opportunity to connect with God.

Pray with a Candle

We light candles as a symbol of our intentions, requests or blessings. A simple ritual of lighting a candle can help us focus on our prayers and can symbolise God, the light of the world. Just remember to blow out the candle when you are finished!

Pray with Simple Triggers

Sometimes we just forget to pray, so 'triggers' can be used to help us remember to take some time to pray. A post-it on your bedroom mirror, an alarm on your phone, a small stone carried in your pocket – it can be anything. Get creative and deliberately place a trigger to remind you to pause and pray.

Pray Online

There are lots of websites, podcasts and apps that can help people to pray. Download some to help you pray and meditate wherever you are.

Pray with the Pope

Before his first blessing, Pope Francis asked people to pray for him. He also encouraged people to pray for others and he explained his 'five finger prayer' to help people remember who to pray for:

1. The thumb is the closest finger to you. So we can start praying for those who are closest to us, like our family and friends. They are the easiest people to remember.

2. The next finger is the index finger. This is the finger we use when we are pointing at things. This finger reminds us to pray for those who teach us, and show us the way. They need the support and wisdom to show direction to others. Always keep them in your prayers.
3. The following finger is the longest. It reminds us of our leaders, and those who have authority. They need God's guidance.
4. The fourth finger is the ring finger. But did you know it is also our weakest finger? It should remind us to pray for the weakest in society, for example those who are sick, poor or in difficulty. They need our prayers.
5. And finally we have our pinkie finger, the smallest of all. This finger should remind you to pray for yourself. When you are done praying for the other four groups,

you will be able to see your own needs but with a sense of perspective, and you will be better able to pray for them.

Pray with Scripture

The Bible is the only book whose author is always present when one reads it. For many centuries a method of prayer known as *Lectio divina* has helped Christians to experience God's Word in the Bible.

Follow these simple steps …

Step 1: Ask the Holy Spirit to Guide You

Invite the Holy Spirit to guide you and give you the grace to hear the words of scripture in all their richness.

Step 2: *Lectio* – Choose a Story from the Bible to Read

To begin, try Matthew 14:22-33. This is the story of Jesus walking on the water as he approaches his disciples who are in the boat. Begin to read the words very slowly, making sure to give this time with God your full attention. Listen to the words with your whole heart and mind.

Step 3: *Meditatio* – Meditate

Take time to meditate and reflect on the words you have read. Remember that all of the stories and books in the Bible sit together to make a whole. Try to understand the meaning of the words. Meditate on them for a while and see if you can apply them to your own life. Does the story encourage or challenge you? Is it asking you to look at some part of your life and to make changes? Listen to what God is saying to you today through these words.

Step 4: *Oratio* – Respond to God

Take time to respond to what you have read.

What comes into your mind in response to this piece of scripture? Thank God for any insight that has come to you and any awareness of God's presence that you feel. Ask God's help with any changes you wish to make in your life.

Step 5: Promise!

Promise to act on your thoughts, and remember your conversation with God today.

For suggested scripture passages to use, see page 186.

Pray without CEASING

1. THESSALONIANS 5:17

SOME PRAYERS TO KNOW BY HEART

It is always useful to know some common prayers off by heart; this makes it easy for us to pray with others. The prayers here are often used during communal prayer at Mass, during school liturgies, at weddings and at funerals. They are short and easy to remember so we can pray them often throughout our life.

The Sign of the Cross
In the name of the Father,
and of the Son,
and of the Holy Spirit.
Amen.

Our Father (The Lord's Prayer)
Our Father who art in heaven,
hallowed be thy name;
Thy kingdom come
thy will be done
on earth as it is in heaven.
Give us this day our daily bread
and forgive us our trespasses
as we forgive those who trespass against us.
And lead us not into temptation,
but deliver us from evil.
Amen.

Hail Mary
Hail Mary, full of grace,
the Lord is with thee.
Blessed art thou among women
and blessed is the fruit of thy womb, Jesus.
Holy Mary, mother of God,
pray for us sinners,
now, and at the hour of our death.
Amen.

Glory Be to the Father
Glory be to the Father,
and to the Son,
and to the Holy Spirit;
As it was in the beginning,
is now, and ever shall be,
world without end.
Amen.

Act of Contrition

O my God, I thank you for loving me.
I am sorry for all my sins,
for not loving others and not loving you.
Help me to live like Jesus and not sin again.
Amen.

Angel of God

Angel sent by God to guide me,
Be my light and walk beside me;
Be my guardian and protect me;
On the paths of life direct me.

Come Holy Spirit
Come, Holy Spirit,
fill the hearts of your faithful.
And kindle in them the fire of your love.
Send forth your Spirit
and they shall be created.
And you shall renew the face of the earth.
Amen.

The Jesus Prayer
Lord Jesus Christ,
Son of God,
have mercy on me,
a sinner.

DAILY PRAYERS

Praying on a daily basis helps to strengthen our relationship with God. We can pray anytime, but it is always nice to centre our day on God with a morning prayer to start our day and a night prayer to end it. If we also say a short prayer before meals we will be keeping in touch with God throughout the day.

Morning Prayers

Lord, help me to remember that nothing is
going to happen to me today that you and I
together can't handle. Amen.

ℓℓℓℓℓℓ

Father in heaven, you love me,
you're with me night and day.
I want to love you always
in all I do and say.
I'll try to please you, Father,
bless me through the day. Amen.

ℓℓℓℓℓℓ

Today is My Day

Today is my day. Today is the day I put aside
all that worried or upset me yesterday.

Today is the day I say 'no' to any thought,
any feeling, any remembrance of past
hurt or disappointment.

Today is the day I say 'yes' to life.

Today is the day I see that I can do more, be
more, live more.

Today is the day I know that neither my
happiness nor my success depend on
any person, place, or thing.

Today is the day I see in myself all the
qualities I need to be happy, to be
fulfilled, to be successful in all that I
undertake.

Today my world is fresh and new.

Today I am filled with self-confidence, with
the assurance that I am the master of my
life.

Today I set about to accomplish
    great things, to live up to the high
    expectations I have for myself.
Today I will succeed, for God is with me and
    his Spirit in me is my inspiration and my
    capability.
Today is my day!

DR BARBARA KING

Dear God,
Today I woke up.
I'm healthy.
I'm alive.
I'm blessed.
I apologise for all my complaining.
I'm truly grateful for all you have done for
    me.

AUTHOR UNKNOWN

Beginning the Day

I'm in a rush, God,
but please stick by me today
to guide me,
to help me.
Support me all the day
with your everlasting love.
Thanks God, for when you're beside me,
I know all will be well.

ROSEMARY AND PETER ATKINS

I Will Be Busy

O Lord,
you know how busy I must be this day.
If I forget you,
do not forget me.

SIR JACOB ASTLEY OF READING
before the Battle of Edgehill, 1642

Dear God,
So far today I've done all right.
I haven't gossiped.
I haven't lost my temper.
I haven't been greedy, grumpy, nasty, selfish
    or overindulgent.
I'm very thankful for that.
But in a few minutes, God, I'm going to get
    out of bed …
And from then on,
I'm probably going to need a lot more help.
Amen.
                    AUTHOR UNKNOWN

Prayers Before Meals
Bless us, O God, as we sit together.
Bless the food we eat today.
Bless the hands that made the food.
Bless us, O God. Amen.

ꙥꙥꙥꙥꙥ

Bless us O Lord,
and these, thy gifts,
which of thy bounty we are about to receive,
through Christ our Lord. Amen.

Night Prayers

God, our Father, I come to say
thank you for your love today.
Thank you for my family
and all the friends you give to me.
Guard me in the dark of night,
and in the morning send your light. Amen.

As I lay me down to sleep,
I pray to God my soul to keep.
And if I die before I wake,
I pray to God my soul to take.
Keep me safe throughout the night,
and wake me with your morning light.
Amen.

The Daily Examen

A great way to pray is to look for God's presence in your life. Saint Ignatius of Loyola encouraged prayer-filled mindfulness by proposing what has been called the Daily Examen. This is a technique of prayerful reflection on the events of the day in order to detect God's presence and to discern God's direction for us. Try this version of St Ignatius's prayer.

1. Become aware of God's presence.
Look back on the events of the day in the company of the Holy Spirit. The day may seem confusing to you – a blur, a jumble, a muddle. Ask God to bring clarity and understanding.

2. Review the day with gratitude.
Gratitude is the foundation of our relationship with God. Walk through your

day in the presence of God and note its joys and delights. Focus on the day's gifts. Look at the work you did, the people you interacted with. What did you receive from these people? What did you give them? Pay attention to small things – the food you ate, the sights you saw, and other seemingly small pleasures. God is in the details.

3. Pay attention to your emotions. One of St Ignatius's great insights was that we detect the presence of the Spirit of God in the movements of our emotions. Reflect on the feelings you experienced during the day. Boredom? Elation? Resentment? Compassion? Anger? Confidence? What is God saying through these feelings?

God will most likely show you some ways in which you fell short. Make note of these sins and faults. But look deeply for other implications. Does a feeling of frustration perhaps mean that God wants you to consider a new direction in some area of your life? Are you concerned about a friend? Perhaps you should reach out to them in some way.

4. Choose one feature of the day and pray about it. Ask the Holy Spirit to direct you to something during the day that God thinks is particularly important. It may involve a feeling – positive or negative. It may be a significant encounter with another person or a vivid moment of happiness or peace. Or it may be something that seems rather insignificant. Look at it. Pray about it. Allow the prayer to flow spontaneously from your heart.

5. Look towards tomorrow. Ask God to give you light for tomorrow's challenges.

Pay attention to the feelings that surface as you survey what's coming up. Are you doubtful? Cheerful? Apprehensive? Allow these feelings to turn into prayer. Seek God's guidance. Ask him for help and understanding. Pray for hope.

Saint Ignatius encouraged people to talk to Jesus like a friend. End the Daily Examen with a conversation with Jesus. Ask forgiveness for your sins. Ask for protection and help. Ask for wisdom about the questions you have and the problems you face. Do all this in the spirit of gratitude. Your life is a gift, and it is adorned with gifts from God.

Come to me, all you that are weary and are carrying heavy burdens, and **I WILL GIVE YOU** **REST**

MATTHEW 11:28

PRAYERS FOR MASS

The Mass is a very special form of prayer. It is a time to praise and worship God. The word Eucharist literally means thanksgiving. There is no better way to spend time with Jesus than by going to Mass and receiving Communion. After all, Jesus clearly asked his followers to 'Do this in memory of me'. During Mass we can say formal prayers with the gathered community, and we remember that Jesus said: 'For where two or three are gathered together in my name, there am I in the midst of them.' We can also take time to say our own private prayers during the Mass, especially after receiving Communion.

Confiteor

I confess to almighty God
and to you, my brothers and sisters,
that I have greatly sinned,
in my thoughts and in my words,
in what I have done and in what I have
    failed to do,
through my fault, through my fault,
through my most grievous fault;
therefore I ask blessed Mary ever-Virgin,
all the Angels and Saints,
and you, my brothers and sisters,
to pray for me to the Lord our God.

The Nicene Creed

I believe in one God,
the Father almighty,
maker of heaven and earth,
of all things visible and invisible.
I believe in one Lord Jesus Christ,
the Only Begotten Son of God,
born of the Father before all ages.

God from God, Light from Light,
true God from true God,
begotten, not made, consubstantial with
the Father;
through him all things were made.
For us men and for our salvation
he came down from heaven,
and by the Holy Spirit was incarnate of the
Virgin Mary,
and became man.
For our sake he was crucified under Pontius
Pilate,
he suffered death and was buried,
and rose again on the third day
in accordance with the Scriptures.
He ascended into heaven
and is seated at the right hand of the
Father.
He will come again in glory
to judge the living and the dead
and his kingdom will have no end.

I believe in the Holy Spirit, the Lord, the
    giver of life,
who proceeds from the Father and the Son,
who with the Father and the Son is adored
    and glorified,
who has spoken through the prophets.
I believe in one, holy, catholic and apostolic
    Church.
I confess one Baptism for the forgiveness of
    sins
and I look forward to the resurrection of the
    dead
and the life of the world to come. Amen

*Sometimes the Apostles' Creed is said
    instead – see pages 47–8.*

Prayer Before Communion

Lord Jesus, come to me.
Lord Jesus, give me your love.
Lord Jesus, come to me and give me
    yourself.

Lord Jesus, friend of children, come to me.
Lord Jesus, you are my Lord and my God.
Praise to you, Lord Jesus Christ.

Prayer After Communion

Lord Jesus, I love and adore you.
You're a special friend to me.
Welcome, Lord Jesus, O welcome.
Thank you for coming to me.

Thank you, Lord Jesus, O thank you
for giving yourself to me.
Make me strong to show your love
wherever I may be.

Be near me, Lord Jesus, I ask you to stay
close by me forever and love me, I pray.
Bless all of us children in your loving care
and bring us to heaven to live with you
    there.

I'm ready now, Lord Jesus,
to show how much I care.
I'm ready now to give your love
at home and everywhere. Amen.

The Gloria is also said at Mass – see pages
    116–17.

PRAYING WITH OUR LADY

Mary has a special role in Catholic tradition – she leads people closer to Jesus. We can pray to Jesus through Mary. The most popular prayer to Our Lady is the Hail Mary, which is on page 22. Mary cares for us as our loving Mother. As Blessed Mother Teresa said: 'If you ever feel distressed during your day – call upon our Lady – just say this simple prayer: "Mary, Mother of Jesus, please be a Mother to me now."'

The Rosary

Saying the Rosary is a way of sharing in the memories of Mary, the Mother of God, and in the memories of the friends of Jesus. It can give you a chance to be with God, with Jesus and with Mary in a quiet, contemplative way. Repeating the Hail Mary ten times (with the Glory Be to the Father and the Our Father in between) can help you to find a quiet space inside yourself. It gives you an opportunity to learn from Jesus, to become like Jesus, to pray to Jesus and to celebrate Jesus.

Different themes or mysteries are used to pray the Rosary on different days. The Rosary can also be a form of meditation – as you pray you can use your imagination to picture and reflect on the events connected with each mystery.

The **Five Joyful Mysteries** are traditionally prayed on the Mondays, Saturdays and Sundays of Advent:

1. The Annunciation
2. The Visitation
3. The Nativity
4. The Presentation in the Temple
5. The Finding in the Temple

The **Five Sorrowful Mysteries** are traditionally prayed on the Tuesdays, Fridays and Sundays of Lent:

1. The Agony in the Garden
2. The Scourging at the Pillar
3. The Crowning with Thorns
4. The Carrying of the Cross
5. The Crucifixion and Death

The **Five Glorious Mysteries** are traditionally prayed on the Wednesdays and Sundays outside of Lent and Advent:

1. The Resurrection
2. The Ascension
3. The Descent of the Holy Spirit
4. The Assumption
5. The Coronation of Mary

The **Five Luminous Mysteries** are traditionally prayed on Thursdays:

1. The Baptism of Christ in the Jordan
2. The Wedding Feast at Cana
3. Jesus' Proclamation of the Coming of the Kingdom of God
4. The Transfiguration
5. The Institution of the Eucharist

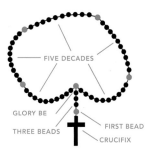

FIVE DECADES

GLORY BE

THREE BEADS

FIRST BEAD

CRUCIFIX

ROSARY BEADS

Praying the Rosary

1. Make the Sign of the Cross.
2. Holding the crucifix, say the Apostles' Creed:

I believe in God,
the Father almighty,
Creator of heaven and earth,
and in Jesus Christ, his only Son, our Lord,
who was conceived by the Holy Spirit,
born of the Virgin Mary,

suffered under Pontius Pilate,
was crucified, died and was buried;
he descended into hell;
on the third day he rose again from the dead;
he ascended into heaven,
and is seated at the right hand of God the
     Father almighty;
from there he will come to judge the living
     and the dead.

I believe in the Holy Spirit,
the holy catholic Church,
the communion of saints,
the forgiveness of sins,
the resurrection of the body,
and life everlasting. Amen.

3. On the first bead, say an Our Father
    (page 21).
4. Say three Hail Marys (page 22) on each
    of the next three beads.

5. Say the Glory Be to the Father (page 22).
6. For each of the five decades, announce the Mystery, then say the Our Father.
7. While moving along each of the ten beads of the decade, say ten Hail Marys while meditating on the Mystery. Then say a Glory Be to the Father.
8. After finishing each decade, say the following prayer:

O my Jesus, forgive us our sins, save us from the fires of hell, lead all souls to heaven, especially those who have most need of your mercy.

9. After saying the five decades, say the Hail, Holy Queen (also known as The *Salve Regina*):

Hail, holy Queen, mother of mercy;
Hail our life, our sweetness, and our hope.

To you we cry, poor banished children of Eve;
to you we send up our sighs,
mourning and weeping in this valley of tears.
Turn, then, most gracious advocate,
your eyes of mercy toward us;
and after this, our exile,
show unto us the blessed fruit of your
    womb, Jesus.
O clement, O loving, O sweet Virgin Mary.

10. Finish with this dialogue and prayer:

Pray for us, O Holy Mother of God.
That we may be made worthy of the
    promises of Christ.

Let us pray:
O God, whose Only Begotten Son,
by his life, Death, and Resurrection,
has purchased for us the rewards of eternal
    life,

grant, we beseech thee,
that while meditating on these mysteries
of the most holy Rosary of the Blessed
    Virgin Mary,
we may imitate what they contain
and obtain what they promise,
through the same Christ our Lord. Amen.

The Angelus

*The Angelus is traditionally said three times
daily, at six in the morning, noon and six in
the evening, but you can pray it anytime.*

The angel of the Lord declared unto Mary
And she conceived by the Holy Spirit.
Hail Mary …

Behold the handmaid of the Lord.
Be it done to me according to your word.
Hail Mary …

And the Word was made flesh
And dwelt among us.
Hail Mary …

Pray for us, O holy Mother of God
That we may be made worthy
of the promises of Christ.

Let us pray:
Pour forth, we beseech thee, O Lord,
thy grace into our hearts,
that we, to whom the incarnation of Christ,
    thy Son,
was made known by the message of an
    angel
may, by his passion and cross,
be brought to the glory of his resurrection,
through the same Christ our Lord.
Amen.

BLESSED
are those who have not
SEEN
and yet have come to
BELIEVE

JOHN 20:29

PRAYING WITH THE SAINTS

S aints are human beings with strengths and weaknesses like everyone else, but what sets them apart is that they discovered God's purpose for their life and used their gifts and talents for the good of others. We can be inspired by the saints to follow their example and discover our true selves. We can pray to the saints to intercede on our behalf and can call on different saints to help us depending on our needs. As St Teresa of Ávila said, 'For prayer is nothing else than being on terms of friendship with God.'

St Thérèse's Prayer

May today there be peace within.

May you trust God that you are exactly
    where you are meant to be.

May you not forget the infinite possibilities
    that are born of faith.

May you use those gifts that you have
    received, and pass on the love that has
    been given to you.

May you be content knowing you are a
    child of God.

Let this presence settle into your bones,

and allow your soul the freedom to sing,
    dance, praise and love.

It is there for each and every one of us.

ATTRIBUTED TO ST THÉRÈSE OF LISIEUX

The Peace Prayer of St Francis of Assisi

Lord, make me an instrument of your peace.
Where there is hatred, let me sow love;
Where there is injury, pardon;
Where there is doubt, faith;
Where there is despair, hope;
Where there is darkness, light;
And where there is sadness, joy.
O Divine Master, grant that I may not so
    much seek
To be consoled as to console;
To be understood as to understand;
To be loved as to love.
For it is in giving that we receive;
It is in pardoning that we are pardoned;
It is in self-forgetting that we find;
And it is in dying that we are born to
    eternal life.
Amen.

An Inspirational Prayer

Do not look forward to what may happen
     tomorrow;
the same everlasting Father who cares
for you today will take care of you
     tomorrow and every day.
Either He will shield you from suffering,
or He will give you unfailing strength to
     bear it.
Be at peace, then.
Put aside all anxious thoughts and
     imaginations,
and say continually: 'The Lord is my
     strength and my shield.
My heart has trusted in Him and I am
     helped.
He is not only with me but in me, and I in
     Him.'

ST FRANCIS DE SALES

The Prayer of St Patrick

I arise today
through the strength of heaven;
light of the sun,
splendour of fire,
speed of lightning,
swiftness of the wind,
depth of the sea,
stability of the earth,
firmness of the rock.

I arise today
through God's strength to pilot me;
God's might to uphold me,
God's wisdom to guide me,
God's eye to look before me,
God's ear to hear me,
God's word to speak for me,
God's hand to guard me,
God's way to lie before me,
God's shield to protect me,
God's hosts to save me

Afar and anear,
Alone or in a multitude.

Christ shield me today
Against wounding
Christ with me, Christ before me, Christ
behind me,
Christ in me, Christ beneath me, Christ
above me,
Christ on my right, Christ on my left,
Christ when I lie down, Christ when I sit
down,
Christ in the heart of everyone who thinks
of me,
Christ in the mouth of everyone who speaks
of me,
Christ in the eye that sees me,
Christ in the ear that hears me.

I arise today
through the mighty strength
of the Lord of creation.

Prayer to St Brigid

You were a woman of peace.
You brought harmony where there was
    conflict.
You brought light to the darkness.
You brought hope to the downcast.
May the mantle of your peace
cover those who are troubled and anxious,
and may peace be firmly rooted in our
    hearts and in our world.
Inspire us to act justly and to reverence all
    God has made.
Brigid you were a voice for the wounded
    and the weary.
Strengthen what is weak within us.
Calm us into a quietness that heals and
    listens.
May we grow each day into greater
wholeness in mind, body and spirit.
Amen.

St Teresa's Prayer

Christ has no body but yours,
no hands, no feet on earth but yours.
Yours are the eyes with which he looks
  compassion on this world.
Yours are the feet with which he walks to do
  good.
Christ has no body now on earth but yours.
Yours are the hands, with which he blesses
  all the world.
Yours are the hands, yours are the feet,
yours are the eyes, you are his body.
Christ has no body now but yours,
no hands, no feet on earth but yours,
Yours are the eyes with which he looks
  compassion on this world.

ST TERESA OF ÁVILA

Knowing, Loving and Serving You

Eternal God,

who are the light of the minds that you
    know,

the joy of the hearts that love you,

and the strength of the wills that serve you;

grant us so to know you

that we may truly love you,

and so to love you

that we may fully serve you,

whom to serve is perfect freedom,

in Jesus Christ our Lord.

ST AUGUSTINE

Prayer of St Anselm

O Lord my God.
Teach my heart this day
where and how to find you.
You have made me and re-made me,
and you have bestowed on me
all the good things I possess,
and still I do not know you.
I have not yet done
that for which I was made.
Teach me to seek you,
for I cannot seek you
unless you teach me,
or find you
unless you show yourself to me.
Let me seek you in my desire;
let me desire you in my seeking.
Let me find you by loving you;
let me love you when I find you

Persistence in Prayer

If God seems at times to be slow in responding, it is because he is preparing a better gift. He will not deny us. We well know that the long-awaited gift is all the more precious for the delay in its being granted ... Ask, seek, insist. Through this asking and seeking you will be better prepared to receive God's gift when it comes. God withholds what you are not yet ready for. He wants you to have a lively desire for his greatest gifts. All of which is to say, pray always and do not lose heart.

ST AUGUSTINE

Prayer to St Anthony

If you lose something you might like to call on St Anthony:

'St Anthony please look all around, my .... is lost and can't be found. Amen.'

A Novena Rose Prayer to St Thérèse of Lisieux

Traditionally a novena is a prayer that people say for nine days in a row for a special intention. There are many novenas to different saints. The one on the next page is to St Thérèse of Lisieux. Saint Thérèse of Lisieux is also known as St Thérèse of the Child Jesus, or is affectionately known as 'The Little Flower' because she said, 'After my death, I will let fall a shower of roses. I will spend my heaven doing good upon earth.' She is very popular because her spirituality is simple and she calls it her 'little way'. She teaches us that life presents enough challenges and opportunities for grace. She teaches us that God is everywhere – in every situation and person – and in the ordinary, simple details of life.

Say this prayer for nine days in a row for a special intention.

O Little Thérèse of the Child Jesus, please pick for me a rose from the heavenly gardens and send it to me as a message of love.
O Little Flower of Jesus, ask God today to grant the favours I now place with confidence in your hands … [mention specific requests]

St Thérèse, help me to always believe as you did, in God's great love for me, so that I might imitate your 'little way' each day.
Amen.

I came
that they may have
Life
and have it
ABUNDANTLY

JOHN 10:10

PRAYERS TO BE THE BEST WE CAN BE

The Bible tells us that God wants us to have full and happy lives. In order to do this we have to play our part by doing our best to become all that we were created to be. As St Catherine of Siena said: 'Be who God meant you to be and you will set the world on fire.'

Aim at Ever Greater Heights

In the world of spiritual endeavour;
as in the world of athletic competition,
we must learn never to be content
with the level we have reached
but, with the help of God
and with our own determined efforts,
we must aim at ever greater heights,
at continual improvement,
so that we may in the end reach maturity,
'the measure of the stature
of the fullness of Christ'.

ST JOHN XXIII

A Missionary Prayer
Let me try a little harder,
let me pray a little more.
Let me go a little farther
than I've ever gone before.
Let me sing instead of sighing
as I pass beneath the rod.
Let my life burn out for others
Less of self and more of God.

LORETO PRAYER BOOK

I Have a Mission
God has made me for a special reason.
Something has been given to me,
which God has given to no one else.
I have my mission.
I may not know everything about it now;
but one day I will look back on life and see
    what it was.
God has not created me for nothing.
No matter who or what I am, I can never be
    put away.

Even if I am sick or unwell, I can do God's
work.

God's plans always work out.

God knows the right thing.

My friends may be gone.

The only people around me may be
strangers.

I may feel depressed.

I may worry about the future.

Still God knows what is right.

So, I will trust in God.

Based on a prayer by

JOHN HENRY CARDINAL NEWMAN

Present

If I searched the highest mountain,
swam the deepest sea,
nothing could compare
to the love you have for me.
Nestled deep within me,
from the time when I began,
your embrace of love and beauty
helps me be the best I can.
Although times I have thought it dormant,
times I could not see,
times I began to lose all hope
that you are there for me.
But I've learned as I get older
that yes! Faith, hope and love are a must,
but I need to be present to you,
And in you always trust.

ORLA WALSH

Strength

Dear God,

Be the strength in others' words that they
may be kind and honest with no intent to
steal the spirit of others.

Be the strength in my words that they
do not willingly hurt others just as I have
wished them not to hurt me.

It comforts me to know that You have such
far-reaching, kind-hearted, Fatherly love for
us.

Even in this networked world we live in,
Your love knows no limit.
Help me keep logged into Your powerful
love and signed out from harshness to
others.
Amen.

AUTHOR UNKNOWN

Discipleship

Send me.

But where, Lord? Send me to do what?

To bring peace where there has been pain
in a person I had not noticed along my daily
path.

To help turn doubt into faith in a person
with whom I eat lunch and have fun.

To bring joy to a life filled up with sadness.

Send me. Send me next door into the next
room,

to speak somehow to a human heart
beating alongside mine.

Send me to bring joy where there is none.

LORETO PRAYER BOOK

May I Become

May I become a light for those in darkness,
a source of hope for those in despair,
a companion for those who are burdened,
a peacemaker for those gripped with anger,
a selfless giver for those who are without,
a compassionate friend for those who
    mourn,
a protector for those without protection,
a bridge for those separated from love.
From this day onwards, may I become fully
    human, fully alive.

PRAYER FOR CATHOLIC SCHOOLS WEEK 2012

The Road Ahead

My Lord God, I have no idea where I am going. I do not see the road ahead of me. I cannot know for certain where it will end. Nor do I really know myself, and the fact that I think that I am following your will does not mean that I am actually doing so. But I believe that the desire to please you does in fact please you. And I hope I have that desire in all that I am doing. I hope that I will never do anything apart from that desire. And I know that if I do this you will lead me by the right road, though I may know nothing about it. Therefore I will trust you always though I may seem to be lost and in the shadow of death. I will not fear, for you are ever with me, and you will never leave me to face my perils alone.

THOMAS MERTON

'Do Not Kill' – And Attention to the Small Things in Life

Loving Lord,
I often see on the TV
news examples of inhumanity to others
– people being tortured, abused,
injured or killed.
I need to remind myself
that the commandment
'do not kill'
also refers to my attitude
and what I do each day,
because it is in smaller ways
that I can destroy people
if I ignore them
or cut them off
or do them down.
Loving Lord, inspire me
to take care of the smaller things of life
as well as the bigger issues. Amen.

AUTHOR UNKNOWN

Do not let your Hearts be troubled and do not let them be afraid.

JOHN 14:27

IN TIMES OF DIFFICULTY

The phrase 'do not be afraid' is written in the Bible three-hundred-and-sixty-five times. That's a daily reminder from God to live every day being fearless. So when times are tough and we face difficulties we can trust in God. Oswald Chambers advised 'we have to pray with our eyes on God, not on our difficulties'. Sometimes we have to pray hardest when it is hardest to pray. When life gives you more than you can stand … kneel.

Guide Me

Guide me through this darkness, Lord.

Hover over me especially when I cannot
seem to hold on for another moment.

Flood me with the graces of hope and
fortitude.

Send your angels to watch over me as I
sleep through the night.

Remind me during the day that from this
small dark cocoon, I will emerge a
butterfly.

CAROLINE MYSS

Jesus, Keep Me Loving

Jesus, I lost it today
and now I am both furious and
embarrassed.
Let me tell you …

What would you have said, Jesus?
How would you have handled it?
I suppose love would have been your guide
but that was not how it was with me.

Lord Jesus, teach me how to love,
to say to others words I could hear from
    them,
to judge others in the way you
would judge me,
with understanding and with love.

ROSEMARY AND PETER ATKINS

Crisis, Lord
I'm in a crisis, Lord
and it's like this

....

Now I've told you,
I'm beginning to feel better.

Dear God, be near me,
to calm me,
to clear my mind,
to take away my fear
and to show me the options
    to move forward.

Give me your strength and wisdom, God,
for you are my friend and my guide.
ROSEMARY AND PETER ATKINS

The Serenity Prayer

God grant me the serenity
to accept the things I cannot change;
courage to change the things I can;
and wisdom to know the difference.
Living one day at a time;
Enjoying one moment at a time;
Accepting hardships as the pathway to
    peace;
Taking, as You did, this sinful world
as it is, not as I would have it;
Trusting that You will make all things right
if I surrender to Your Will;
That I may be reasonably happy in this life
and supremely happy with You
Forever in the next.
Amen.

ATTRIBUTED TO REINHOLD NIEBUHR

A Prayer for Our Journey With Jesus

Jesus, in You
I am never alone,
even at difficult moments,
even when my life's
journey comes up against
problems and obstacles
that seem insurmountable.
I accompany You,
I follow You,
but above all
I know that You
accompany me and
carry me on Your shoulders.
This is my joy, this is the hope
that I must bring to this world.
Teach me to see
with Your eyes,
to live life as You lived,
to understand life
as You understood it.

Help me be ready for an
encounter with You,
which means being able
to see the signs of
Your presence,
keeping my faith alive with
prayer and the sacraments,
and taking care
not to forget about God.

POPE FRANCIS

For Perseverance Today

If things get tough today, Lord – and in all hard times – let me stay motivated and calm. Let me look at how far I have come rather than how far I still have to go. Let me continue counting my blessings, not what I've been missing. May every day bring new chances to grow, new beautiful things to see, new plans to do, and new goals to pursue, as every new day is Your miracle day.

AUTHOR UNKNOWN

WHEN WE LOSE SOMEONE WE LOVE

When we lose someone we love our faith can be rocked. Often when someone dies, the people around us are also dealing with this loss and may react differently to us. We need to be kind and patient with ourselves and others. It is okay to be angry with God; it is okay to ask why. It is okay to scream and cry. The Bible tells us, 'Tears are prayers too. They travel to God when we can't speak' (see Psalm 56:8). We can find comfort in our faith, especially in the belief of eternal life in heaven. This can give us the strength to go on as we have hope that we will be reunited with our loved ones again.

Blessed are those who mourn, for they will
be comforted.

MATTHEW 5:4

The Ship
What is dying?
I am standing on the seashore.
A ship sails to the morning breeze and
    starts for the ocean.
She is an object and I stand watching her
till at last she fades from the horizon,
And someone at my side says, 'She is
    gone!' Gone where?
Gone from my sight, that is all;
she is just as large in the masts, hull and
    spars as she was when I saw her,
and just as able to bear her load of living
    freight to its destination.
The diminished size and total loss of sight is
    in me, not in her;
and just at the moment when someone at
    my side says, 'She is gone',

There are others who are watching her
    coming,
And other voices take up a glad shout,
'There she comes' – and that is dying.

BISHOP CHARLES HENRY BRENT (1862–1929)

He is Gone

You can shed tears that he is gone
or you can smile because he has lived.

You can close your eyes and pray that he
    will come back
or you can open your eyes and see all he
    has left.

Your heart can be empty because you can't
    see him
or you can be full of the love that you
    shared.

You can turn your back on tomorrow and
    live yesterday
or you can be happy for tomorrow because
    of yesterday.

You can remember him and only that he is
    gone
or you can cherish his memory and let it live
    on.
You can cry and close your mind, be empty
    and turn your back
or you can do what he'd want: smile, open
    your eyes, love and go on.

DAVID HARKINS

Farewell My Friends
It was beautiful
as long as it lasted
the journey of my life.
I have no regrets
whatsoever save

the pain I'll leave behind.
Those dear hearts
who love and care …
and the heavy with sleep
ever moist eyes.
The smile, in spite of a
lump in the throat
and the strings pulling
at the heart and soul.
The strong arms
that held me up
when my own strength
let me down.
Each morsel that I was fed
with was full of love.
At every turning of my life
I came across good friends.
Friends who stood by me
even when time raced by.
Farewell, farewell
my friends.

I smile and bid you goodbye.
No, shed no tears,
for I need them not
All I need is your smile.
If you feel sad
think of me
for that's what I'd like.
When you live in the hearts
of those you love,
remember then …
you never die.

GITANJALI GHEI

When the righteous cry for help, the Lord
    hears,
and rescues them from all their troubles.
The Lord is near to the broken-hearted,
and saves the crushed in spirit.

PSALM 34:17-18

Lord, Welcome Those Who Have Died

Lord,
welcome into your calm and peaceful
    kingdom
those who have departed out of this
    present life to be with you.
Grant them rest
and a place with the spirits of the just;
and give them the life that knows no age,
the reward that passes not away,
through Christ our Lord. Amen.

ST IGNATIUS LOYOLA

Till the Shades Lengthen

May the Lord support us all the day long
till the shades lengthen
and the evening comes,
and the busy world is hushed,
and the fever of life is over
and our work is done.

Then, in his mercy,
may he give us a safe lodging and a holy
    rest
and peace at the last.

JOHN HENRY CARDINAL NEWMAN

Why Some So Young?

I have been to funerals before
Funerals of family and family friends,
Funerals for people I knew and loved and
    grieved for.
But this is different,
This is someone young
And that scares me.
I can't make any sense out of it.
Why does someone so young and full of life
    have to die?
How could you let this happen?
Don't you know how much pain this causes?

I can't escape thinking about death now.

I am faced with the reality that I might not
    live until I am old and grey.
I have to accept that life is short
and no one knows what is going to happen
    in the future.
Only one thing is certain, we will all die.
Please help me to process this reality
so that I can make the most of the life that
    I have.
Help me find comfort in the belief that one
    day
I will be reunited with my loved ones who
    have gone before me.
Help me to discover meaning and purpose
    in my life,
so that I may live fully while I am alive.
Help me to cherish each moment of my life
    and all those I love,
taking nothing for granted.
Amen.

AILÍS TRAVERS

As the Heavens Open
As the heavens open
And the rain pours down,
Never do I picture or see your frown.
Your smile glows so strong and bright
You're up in heaven with God at night.

You keep us well, safe and free
You guide us when we cannot see.

God walks with us and so do you,
In thick and thin he sees us through.

We let God know how grateful we are
For the time we had with you.

AMY HUGHES

Eternal Rest
Eternal rest grant unto them, O Lord.
And let perpetual light shine upon them.
May they rest in peace.
Amen.

PRAYERS OF PETITION

In prayers of petition we ask God for any physical or spiritual things we need. It makes sense to pray these in our own words when possible, and when you can't put your prayer into words, God hears your heart. Anytime we pray, God hears more than we say, answers more than we ask, gives more than we imagine … in God's own time and own way.

But as for me, I will look to the Lord,
I will wait for the God of my salvation; my
God will hear me.

MICAH 7:7

Angel Sent by God
Angel sent by God to guide me,
be my light and walk beside me,
be my Guardian and protect me,
on the path of life direct me.

Stay With Me Lord
Stay with me Lord Jesus
be my companion on the road;
enkindle my heart and stir up my hope
so that I and all people may learn to know
you in the scripture
and in the breaking of bread.
Amen.

Help in Making Decisions

Lord, I am about to make an important
    decision
and my mind is full of uncertainty.
Help me to feel your presence
with every beat of my heart,
with every smile from my friends,
with every minute that passes.
Help me to make the best decision
for me, for others and for you.
O Lord, hear my prayer.

ORLA WALSH

Faith

Father,
cause my faith to grow
so that through all the circumstances of my
    life
I can, in my struggle,
feel your presence and your love with me.

Hope

Father,
give me the hope
which has seen things at their worst,
and refuses to despair;
which is able to fail and try again;
which can accept disappointment and
sorrow
and find joy in the hope of Resurrection.

Love

Father,
increase my love.
Help me to love people as you love them.
Teach me what love really is,
how much it costs
and the courage needed to achieve it,
today, tomorrow and for the rest of our
lives. LORETO PRAYER BOOK

Lord, Be With Me

Lord,
when I was younger
I didn't really understand you,
but I was filled with your love.

Lord,
when I celebrated my First Holy Communion
I felt I knew you better now,
nourished by your love.

Lord,
when I celebrated my Confirmation
I had developed a relationship with you,
I was empowered by the Holy Spirit.

Lord,
now I am a teenager.
I'm mixed up and confused.
Sometimes I don't feel anything.

Lord,
I ask you to be with me
on this journey of life.
Help me to accept my faith as part of me,
    always.

O Lord, hear my prayer.

AUTHOR UNKNOWN

Cast all your
ANXIETIES
ON HIM
because he
CARES FOR YOU

1 PETER 5:7

PRAYERS OF INTERCESSION

In prayers of intercession we make requests to God on behalf of other people. Blessed Mother Teresa once said, 'I used to believe that prayer changes things, but now I know that prayer changes us and we change things.' God often answers prayers through us, so when we talk to God on behalf of others we can begin to see how we can make a difference in the lives of others. We can pray for others by thinking of them while we say a prayer we know by heart, or just by having a conversation with God about them.

I Said a Prayer for You Today

I said a prayer for you today
and know God must have heard.
I felt the answer in my heart
although he spoke no word

I didn't ask for wealth or fame
(I knew you wouldn't mind).
I asked him to send you treasures
of a far more lasting kind.

I asked that he be near you
at the end of each new day,
to grant you health and blessings
and friends to share your way!

I asked for happiness for you
in all things great and small,
but it was for his loving care
I prayed the most of all!

AUTHOR UNKNOWN

May God Give You
May God give you …
for every storm, a rainbow,
for every tear, a smile,
for every care, a promise,
and a blessing in each trial.
For every problem life sends,
a faithful friend to share,
for every sigh, a sweet song,
and an answer for each prayer.

ANONYMOUS IRISH BLESSING

PRAYERS OF PENITENCE

In prayers of penitence we say sorry to God. When we sin we damage our relationship with God. In the Catholic tradition the Sacrament of Reconciliation is the way we can be fully reconciled to God. It is good to carry out an examination of conscience beforehand to be aware of times that we failed to love God, others and ourselves. During the Sacrament of Reconciliation we will be invited to say the Act of Contrition, which is on page 23. In between attending the Sacrament of Reconciliation we can talk to God about our lives in an honest way, sharing the things that we are not proud of and asking God to help us learn from our mistakes and grow in love.

I loved you at your darkest.

ROMANS 5:8

Examination of Conscience

An examination of conscience is the act of looking prayerfully into our hearts to ask how we have hurt our relationships with God and other people through our thoughts, words and actions. We can reflect on the Ten Commandments and the teachings of the Church to help us in our examination of conscience.

My Relationship With God

What steps am I taking to help me grow closer to God and to others? Do I turn to God often during the day, through good times and bad?

Do I participate at Mass with attention and devotion?

Do I use God's name and the names of Jesus with love and reverence?

My Relationships With Family, Friends and Neighbours

Have I set a bad example through my words or actions? Do I treat others fairly? Do I spread stories that hurt other people?

Am I loving of those in my family? Am I respectful of my neighbours, my friends, and those in authority?

Do I show respect for my body and for the bodies of others? Do I keep away from forms of entertainment that do not respect God's gift of sexuality?

Have I taken or damaged anything that did not belong to me? Have I cheated, copied homework or lied?

Do I quarrel with others just so I can get my own way? Do I insult others to try to make them think they are less than I am? Do I hold grudges and try to hurt people who I think have hurt me?

Your Forgiveness
Your forgiveness is total,
no notebook,
tape recorder,
or post-it note
to remind you of that moment when …
You take our confession,
offered with hands outstretched,
and gently,
like the loving
heavenly Father that you are,
put it to one side
to be forgotten.
No grudges, no itching for judgement,

no resentment or ill-will.
Not like us
who find it easy to say sorry,
but so hard to forgive absolutely.
Forgive us, Father,
that we are often more willing
to accept forgiveness,
than to forgive,
more willing to accept your love,
than to share it with those who have hurt us.
Teach us to forgive,
as you forgive.

JOHN BIRCH

Lord, Strengthen My Morality

God of love and forgiveness,
help me to respect those who are different
 from me,
those who annoy me,
those who make mistakes,
those who always do things their own way,
and those who ignore me even when I am
 trying to be their friend.
Lord, as I bring these requests to you,
I am working at being a better person,
I am trying to grow in morality.
I am searching for patience,
kindness and the ability to forgive,
qualities that will nourish and strengthen my
 moral life.
I ask this through Jesus Christ Our Lord.
Amen.

ORLA WALSH

PRAYERS OF PRAISE, THANKSGIVING, BLESSING AND ADORATION

In these prayers we acknowledge our dependence on God, we express our love for God and we say thank you to God. G. E. Lessing said, 'One single grateful thought raised to heaven is the most perfect prayer', Meister Eckhart said, 'If the only prayer you ever say in your entire life is thank you, it will be enough', and in the Bible it says 'Devote yourselves to prayer, keeping alert in it with thanksgiving' (Colossians 4:2).

Prayer of Thanksgiving

O God,
I thank you for this day of life,
for eyes to see the sky,
for ears to hear the birds,
for feet to walk amidst the trees,
for hands to pick the flowers from the earth,
for a sense of smell to breathe in the sweet
    perfumes of nature,
for a mind to think about and appreciate
the magic of everyday miracles,
for a spirit to swell in joy at Your mighty
    presence everywhere.
Amen.

MARIAN WRIGHT EDELMAN

How Can We Praise You?

How can we praise you
in life's ordinary moments,
bus, car or train,
pedestrian moments,

at home and employment,
with all those distractions.
How can we praise you?

How can we praise you
when time is so precious,
appointments and targets
distracting our focus,
muddying waters,
made clean for your purpose.
How can we praise you?

How can we praise you?
Through all of our actions,
a smile and a greeting,
a shoulder to lean on,
a word in due season,
love and compassion,
in all situations.

JOHN BIRCH

A Song of Praise

Jesus
I am not a poet
or musician
but
I have written
a song of praise
in my heart.
And in the quietness
of this moment
I shall share it with you
in the certain knowledge
that any imperfections
will be made perfect
in the simple act
of opening my heart
and singing.

JOHN BIRCH

The Gloria

Glory to God in the highest,
and on earth peace to people of good will.

We praise you,
we bless you,
we adore you,
we glorify you,
we give you thanks for your great glory,
Lord God, heavenly King,
O God, almighty Father.
Lord Jesus Christ, Only Begotten Son,
Lord God, Lamb of God, Son of the Father,
    you take away the sins of the world,
have mercy on us;
you take away the sins of the world,
receive our prayer;
you are seated at the right hand of the
    Father, have mercy on us.
For you alone are the Holy One,
you alone are the Lord,
you alone are the Most High,
Jesus Christ,
with the Holy Spirit,
in the glory of God the Father

PRAYERS FOR THE WORLD AND CREATION

When we stop and look closely at the world around us we can see the wonder of God's creation. Noticing the beauty of the world can be a reminder of God the creator, how God cares for all of creation, which includes us. We are also reminded that God has given people a special role to care for the earth as we are made in the image and likeness of God.

Look at the birds of the air; they neither sow nor reap nor gather into barns, and yet your heavenly Father feeds them. Are you not of more value than they? And can any of you by worrying add a single hour to your span of life?

MATTHEW 6:26-27

Saint John Paul II Reminds Us of Our Mission to Others

Dear young people,

May you too learn to look at your neighbour and at creation with God's eyes. Mainly respect its summit, which is the human person. At the school of such excellent teachers, learn the careful and attentive use of goods. Do your utmost to see that they are better distributed and shared, with full respect for the rights of every person. In reading the great book of creation, may your spirit open to grateful praise to the Creator.

ST JOHN PAUL II

Geography Prayer

We're grateful for the trees,
the oxygen we breathe,
in the summer red roses bloom,
at the end of the day look up at the moon.
We are worried about our environment,
we all need some enlightenment,
let's stop all the confusion,
let's start a green revolution.
We need to stop and listen,
to our world's petition.
We need to recycle, we need to reuse,
not to waste water, we need to choose.

MR FITZGERALD AND THE STUDENTS OF
LORETO COLLEGE 3B CLASS OF 2014/2015

Growing in Wonder

God our Father,
may the vastness of your creation
that we can begin to see through a telescope,
remind us of the abundance of your love.
May the lowliness
of the smallest creatures and cells
that we can see through a microscope,
remind us of how insignificant – yet special –
we appear to be.
May our vision each day
of the world around us
remind us that you so loved the world
that you sent Jesus, your Son,
to be one of us.
In all that we observe,
open our eyes
so that we may really see
and grow in wonder and appreciation.
Amen.

AUTHOR UNKNOWN

In Praise of Creation

There is glory
within each sunrise, Lord,
a warm effusion of praise
reaching upwards and out,
connecting earth
with heaven,
creator
with created,
Shafts of sunlight,
arms outstretched in worship
encourage participation
from those who watch
and wonder,
at the beauty of it all.

JOHN BIRCH

Respect for All Life

God our Father,
inspire us with a great respect
for all human life
from the time of the child
growing in the womb
to the point of death.
May that respect lead us
to grow in a sense of responsibility
for all our brothers and sisters
throughout the world,
knowing that, where one person suffers
and is degraded,
all of humanity is belittled and abused.
May we grow in a sense of love and care
for those less fortunate than ourselves,
and lead us to do something
about the troubles in our world.
Amen.

AUTHOR UNKNOWN

The Wonderer

I wish that I could understand
The moving marvel of my hand;
I watch my fingers turn and twist,
The supple bending of my wrist,
The dainty touch of finger tip,
The steel intensity of grip;
A tool of exquisite design,

With pride I think: 'It's mine! It's mine!'
Then there's the wonder of my eyes,
Where hills and houses, seas and skies
In waves of light converge and pass,
And print themselves as on a glass.
Line, form and colour live in me;
I am the beauty that I see;
Ah! I could write a book of size
About the wonder of my eyes.

What of the wonder of my heart,
That plays so faithfully its part?

I hear it running sound and sweet;
It does not seem to miss a beat;
Between the cradle and the grave
It never falters, staunch and brave.
Alas! I wish I had the art
To tell the wonder of my heart.

Then, oh! but how can I explain
The wondrous wonder of my brain?
That marvellous machine that brings
All consciousness of wonderings;
That lets me from myself leap out
And watch my body walk about;
It's hopeless – all my words are vain
To tell the wonder of my brain.

But do not think, O patient friend,
Who reads these stanzas to the end,
That I myself would glorify ...
You're just as wonderful as I,
And all Creation is our view

Is quite as marvellous as you.
Come, let us on the seashore stand

And wonder at a grain of sand;
And then into the meadow pass
And marvel at a blade of grass;
Or cast our vision high and far
And thrill with wonder at a star;
A host of stars – night's holy tent
Huge glittering with wonderment.

If wonder is in great and small,
Then what of Him who made it all?
In heart and brain and heart and limb
Let's see the wondrous work of Him.
In house and hill and sward and sea,
In bird and beast and flower and tree,
In everything from sun to sod,
The wonder and the awe of God.

ROBERT W. SERVICE

DO NOT BE AFRAID

for I am your God;

I will strengthen you, I will help you; I will uphold you with my

VICTORIOUS

RIGHT HAND

ISAIAH 41:10

JUSTICE AND PEACE

It is always worth remembering that someone else is praying for the things we take for granted. We live in a world that is full of injustice, violence and suffering but we have hope that God created us with all the ability and potential to make the world a better place. We can pray for justice and peace but that is just the first step. We then must put our faith into action and as Mahatma Gandhi said, 'be the change you want to see in the world'.

Open Our Eyes, Lord
God,
The image of your Son is not visible
in the pages of our newspapers
in the faces of our leaders
in the deployment of our weapons
in the violence of our actions.
Christ,
take our words
our world
our weapons
our work
and transform them in your image.
So we may see your face
in truth where news is reported
in justice where power is abused
in peace where war is threatened
in reconciliation where deeds foster hatred.
Open our eyes, Lord!

WORLD COUNCIL OF CHURCHES

When Working for Charity and Justice

Lord, we ask you to enable us in our work
for charity and justice.

We pray that our efforts may be life-giving
to others,

and that the fruits of our labours offer hope
and stability.

We thank you for our families,

our homes,

our communities

and each other.

We thank you for the opportunity to help
others who have a more difficult life
situation.

We are inspired by the Holy Father [Pope
Benedict XVI] when he said:

Jesus identifies himself with those in
need, with the hungry, the thirsty, the
stranger, the naked, the sick and those in
prison, 'as you did it to one of these my
brethren, you did it to me' (Mt 25:40).

This Gospel passage demonstrates how love of God and love of neighbour have become one: in the least of the brethren we find Jesus himself, and in Jesus we find God.

AUTHOR UNKNOWN

May it Come Soon

May it come soon
to the hungry
to the weeping
to those who thirst for justice,
to those who have waited centuries
for a truly human life.
Grant us the patience
to smooth the way
on which your kingdom comes to us.
Grant us the hope
that we may not weary
in proclaiming and working for it,
despite so many conflicts,

threats and shortcomings.
Grant us a clear vision
that in the hour of our history
we may see the horizon,
and know the way
on which your kingdom comes to us.

PRAYER FOR NICARAGUA

I Believe

I believe in the equality of all, rich and poor.
I believe in liberty.
I believe in humanity and that through it we
    can create unity.
I believe in love within each of us,
and in the home, happy and healthy.
I believe in the forgiveness of our sins.
I believe that with divine help
we will have the strength to establish
    equality in society.
I believe in unity, the only way to achieve
    peace,

and I believe that together we can obtain
  justice.

The *Livesimply* Prayer
Compassionate and loving God,
you created the world for us all to share,
a world of beauty and plenty.
Create in us a desire to live simply,
so that our lives may reflect your generosity.

Creator God,
you gave us responsibility for the earth,
a world of riches and delight.
Create in us a desire to live sustainably,
so that those who follow after us
may enjoy the fruits of your creation.

God of peace and justice,
you give us the capacity to change,
to bring about a world that mirrors your
  wisdom.

Create in us a desire to act in solidarity,
so that the pillars of injustice crumble
and those now crushed are set free.
Amen.

LINDA JONES/CAFOD

A Sabbath Prayer

We cannot merely pray to you, O God, to
   end war;
For we know that You have made the world
   in a way
That man must find his own path to peace.
Within himself and with his neighbour.

We cannot merely pray to You, O God, to
   end starvation;
For You have already given us the resources
With which to feed the entire world,
If we would only use them wisely.

We cannot merely pray to You, O God, to
   root out prejudice;

For You have already given us eyes
With which to see the good in all men,
If we would only use them rightly.

We cannot merely pray to You, O God, to
    end despair,
For You have already given us the power
To clear away slums and to give hope,
If we would only use our power justly.

We cannot merely pray to You, O God, to
    end disease;
For You have already given us great minds
With which to search out cures and healing,
If we would only use them constructively.

Therefore we pray to You instead, O God,
For strength, determination and will power,
To do instead of just pray,
To become instead of merely to wish.

JACK RIEMER

The Eucharistic Congress Prayer

The 50th International Eucharistic Congress was held in Ireland in 2012. This is the official prayer, written for this special occasion.

Lord Jesus,
You were sent by the Father
to gather together those who are scattered.
You came among us, doing good and
    bringing healing,
announcing the Word of salvation
and giving the Bread which lasts forever.
Be our companion on life's pilgrim way.

May your Holy Spirit inflame our hearts,
enliven our hope and open our minds,
so that together with our sisters and
    brothers in faith
we may recognise you in the Scriptures
and in the breaking of bread.
May your Holy Spirit transform us into one
    body

and lead us to walk humbly on the earth,
in justice and love,
as witnesses of your resurrection.

In communion with Mary,
whom you gave to us as our Mother
at the foot of the cross,
through you
may all praise, honour and blessing be to
    the Father
in the Holy Spirit and in the Church,
Now and forever.
Amen

LET NO ONE DESPISE YOUR

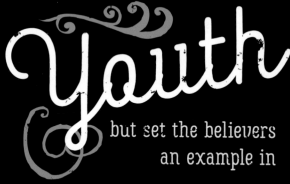

Youth

but set the believers
an example in

SPEECH AND CONDUCT

IN LOVE, IN FAITH

IN PURITY

1 TIMOTHY 4:12

SCHOOL LIFE

Some say our school days are the best days of our life. When we leave school we may look back on our school days fondly but the reality is that they are also days that are filled with pressures and stress and worries. It is not easy preparing for exams and figuring out what we want to do after school. We may also have to deal with friendship issues, peer pressure and bullying along the way. All we can really do is take one day at a time, learning from our mistakes, asking for help when we have problems and doing the best we can to make our school days happy for us and for those around us. As St Francis of Assisi said: 'Start by doing what is necessary, then do what is possible and suddenly you are doing the impossible.'

A Student's Creed

Today, this new day, I am a successful student. Overnight my mind and body have produced thousands of new cells to give me the greatest advantages possible. I am born anew, revitalised, and full of energy.

I am rare and valuable; unique in all the universe. I am nature's greatest miracle in action. I have unlimited potential. I believe in my abilities, attitudes and goals. I am worthy of greatness because I am the most important person in my world.

Today I push myself to new limits. I use my skills and knowledge every day. I begin the day with a success and end it with a success. My goals are being reached every day and I seek them eagerly.

I act positively and happily, fully accepting myself and others. I live to the fullest by experiencing life without limits. I embrace life. I approach each class, each book, and each assignment with enthusiasm, happiness and joy. I thirst for knowledge. I look forward to reading and believing this creed each and every day.

I am a positive and successful student. I know each step I must take to continue to be that way. I am clear on my goals and see myself reaching them. I now realise my infinite potential, thus, my burden lightens. I smile and laugh. I have become the greatest student in the world.

AUTHOR UNKNOWN

For Friendship

May you be blessed with good friends,
And learn to be a good friend to yourself,
Journeying to that place in your soul where
There is love, warmth of feeling.
May this change you.

May it transfigure what is negative, distant
Or cold within your heart.

May you be brought in to real passion, kindness
And belonging.

May you treasure your friends.
May you be good to them, be there for them
And receiving all the challenges, truth and light you need.

May you never be isolated but know the embrace
Of your Anam Ċara.

JOHN O'DONOHUE

Bullying

I saw his frustration, Lord,
as he was bullied again.
He's just a bit smaller than the rest of us,
and seems to bring out the bully in us.
I'd love to take his part but I'm afraid.
I can see girls laughing when it's happening,
but you can see the hurt in their eyes for
    him.
There's a tear in my heart for him.
The mockery is like a crown of thorns on his
    head,
he must dread coming to school.
Why do we pick on weaknesses in people,
    Lord?
I know I have laughed at him sometimes,
and I hate it when people laugh at my
    height.
I know I'm tall but that doesn't make me a
    freak.
I just pray for him now, Lord.

I pray he won't be damaged,
and I pray that I'll do something about it,
either stand up for him,
be friendly to him
or talk to a teacher about it.
Help us, Lord, to build up the good in each
other,
not laugh at the weaknesses.
Some day the bullies will be left alone,
because nobody puts up with loudmouths
forever.
Help them see the light also, Lord,
and give up making life hell for a gentle
person.
Give me the courage, Lord, to change this
situation.
You were a person who stood up for others,
and knew what it was like to be bullied.
Lord, help me to do my best for him,
and help us put an end to the bullying.

DONAL NEARY

Peer Pressure

God I am feeling very confused,
I want to fit in,
and keep the friends that I have made.
But sometimes I feel that if people knew
the real me they wouldn't like me.
I am always wearing a mask.
Trying to be someone I am not to fit in.
I do this so much even I do not know who I
really am anymore.
I have a mask that I wear at home and a
mask that I wear in school
and a whole variety of masks that I wear for
different occasions
But who am I when the masks come off?
How can I just be me, the person you
created me to be?
I don't want to stand out in case people
discover that I am an imposter.
So I go along with the crowd
Letting others make the decisions for me

Doing what everyone else is doing
To fit in
To be liked
But I am afraid one day I will look in the
    mirror and not recognise myself
Who will I become if I do not know myself,
If I do not like myself
If I don't listen to my own inner voice?
God I am feeling very confused,
Help me be free to be myself.

AILÍS TRAVERS

The Athlete's Prayer

God let me play well, but fairly.
Let competition make me strong, but never
  hostile.
In this and in all things, guide me to the
  virtuous path.
If I know victory, grant me happiness.
If I am denied, keep me from envy.
See me not when I am cheered,
but when I bend to help my opponent up.
Seal it in my heart that everyone
who takes the field with me becomes my
  brother.
Remind me that sports are just games.
Teach me something that will matter once
  the games are over.
And if through athletics I set an example –
  let it be a good one.
Amen.

UNKNOWN AUTHOR

Students' Prayers at Exam Time

God of Wisdom, I thank you for the knowledge gained and the learning experiences of this year.

I come to you and ask you to illuminate my mind and heart.

Let your Holy Spirit be with me as I prepare for exams, guiding my studies and giving me insight so that I can perform to the best of my ability.

Please grant me the strength to handle the pressure of these days, the confidence to feel secure in my knowledge, and the ability to keep a proper perspective through it all.

Help me to keep in mind what is truly important, even as I focus my time and energy on these exams.

Finally, may I sense your peace in knowing that I applied myself to the challenges of this day.

I ask this through Christ our Lord. Amen.

AUTHOR UNKNOWN

Creator of all things,
true source of light and wisdom,
origin of all being,
graciously let a ray of your light penetrate
the darkness of my understanding.
Take from me the double darkness
in which I have been born,
an obscurity of sin and ignorance.
Give me a keen understanding,
a retentive memory, and
the ability to grasp things
correctly and fundamentally.
Grant me the talent
of being exact in my explanations
and the ability to express myself
with thoroughness and charm.
Point out the beginning,
direct the progress,
and help in the completion.
I ask this through Christ our Lord.
Amen.

ST THOMAS AQUINAS

Loving God, I turn to you today.

As the exam approaches I am nervous and
so I ask you to help me.

You know how important these exams are
to me.

Set me free from worry, give me your peace
and help me to think clearly.

Help me to remember what I have learned,
to use my time well, not to panic, to
do my best and not to worry about the
outcome.

Help me to realise that the exams are not
there to catch me out but to find out
how much I know.

Lord, keep me calm so that I can write
down all I know!

Keep my friends calm too, we're all in this
together.

Let me sleep each night so that I am
refreshed and renewed for the next
exam.

Even if I struggle I must always remember
that there is a bigger picture of which
these exams are only a small part.
Most important of all, calm me down, keep
me focused,
guide me along, get me through the scary
moments
and make sure I attempt every question.
Thank you for being my friend today and
always. Amen.

AUTHOR UNKNOWN

End of School Year
O God of all beginnings and endings,
We praise and thank you for the gift of this
school year.
It has been a time filled with grace and
blessings,
With challenges and opportunities, joys and
sorrows.

The days have passed quickly, O Lord.
The weeks, the months, the seasons, the
holidays and holy days,
The exams, vacations, breaks and
assemblies,
All have come forth from your hand.

While we trust that your purposes have
always been at work each day,
Sometimes it has seemed difficult to
understand and appreciate
Just what you have been up to in our
school.
Give us the rest and refreshment we need
this summer.
Let our efforts of this past year bear fruit.
Bring all of our plans to a joyful conclusion,
And bless us, according to your will,
With the fulfilment of our summer hopes
and dreams.

Watch over us in the weeks of rest ahead,
And guide each day as you have done this
past year.
Help us return to school with a new spirit
and a new energy.

May we continue to grow
In age, wisdom, knowledge and grace
All the days of our lives.
Amen.

AUTHOR UNKNOWN

Pray as if everything depended on God and
work as if everything depended on you.

ST IGNATIUS OF LOYOLA

St Thomas Aquinas, patron of students,
pray for us.

St Joseph of Cupertino, patron of test
takers, pray for us.

In all your ways acknowledge

HIM

and he will

MAKE
STRAIGHT
YOUR
PATHS

PROVERBS 3:6

REFLECTIONS

God speaks to us through the people around us, through nature, through things that we see, hear and read. Often we find inspiration from our lives in unexpected places. The following reflections give some inspiration for life.

The Cracked Pot

An elderly woman had two large pots. Each hung on the end of a pole, which she carried across her neck. One of the pots had a crack in it while the other pot was perfect and always delivered a full portion of water at the end of the long walk from the stream to the house. The cracked pot always arrived only half full.

For a full two years this went on daily, with the woman bringing home only one-and-a-half pots of water. Of course, the perfect pot was proud of its accomplishments. But the poor cracked pot was ashamed of its own imperfection, and miserable that it could only do half of what it had been made to do.

After two years of what it perceived to be bitter failure, it spoke to the woman one day by the stream, 'I am ashamed of myself, because this crack in my side causes water to leak out all the way back to your house.' The old woman smiled, 'Did you notice that there are flowers on your side of the path, but not on the other pot's side? That's because I have always known about your flaw, so I planted flower seeds on your side of the path, and every day while we walk back, you water them. For two years I have been able to pick these beautiful flowers to decorate the table. Without you being just the way you are, there would not be this beauty to grace the house.'

The moral of this story: each of us has our own unique flaws. We're all cracked pots. In this world, nothing goes to waste. You may think like the cracked pot that you are inefficient or useless in certain areas of your life, but somehow these flaws can turn out to be a blessing in disguise. This kind of story makes you proud of being a cracked pot, doesn't it? Look around and you will see all the lives that you have touched/ watered.

It's the cracks and flaws we each have that make our lives together so very interesting and rewarding. You've just got to take each person for what they are and look for the good in them.

AUTHOR UNKNOWN

You Are Beautiful
Imagine this:
You just painted the most beautiful picture you have ever painted. It is exactly what you wanted. You absolutely love it! But the person you give it to constantly points out the flaws …

How does that make you feel?

God is the painter and you are the masterpiece. It breaks God's heart when you constantly criticise yourself, because God made you perfect.

Footprints

One night a man had a dream.
He dreamed he was walking along the
    beach with the Lord.
Across the sky, flashed scenes from his life.
For each scene, he noticed two sets of
    footprints in the sand;
one belonged to him, the other to the Lord.

When the last scene of his life flashed
    before him,
he looked back at the footprints in the
    sand.
he noticed that many times along the path
    of his life, there was only one set of
    footprints.

He also noticed that it happened at the
lowest and saddest times in his life.
This bothered him and he questioned the
Lord about it.
'Lord, you said that once I decided to follow
you, you'd walk with me all the way.
But I have noticed that during the most
troublesome times in my life,
there is only one set of footprints,
I don't understand why when I needed you
the most, you would leave me.'

The Lord replied,
'My precious, precious child, I love you and
would never leave you.
During the times of trial and suffering, when
you see only one set of footprints,
it was then that I carried you.'

God Doesn't Ask

God doesn't ask if you are an honours or
   pass candidate but asks how you treat
   the people you meet each day.

God doesn't ask who designed your clothes
   but asks how many people you care for
   each day.

God doesn't ask how much money you have
   but asks if you earned it honestly and
   spent it wisely.

God doesn't ask what result you got in your
   last exam but asks if you performed to
   the best of your ability.

God doesn't ask how many friends you have
   but asks how many you have been a
   friend to.

God doesn't ask what your address is but
   asks how you treat your neighbours.

God doesn't ask about the colour of your
   skin but asks about the content of your
   character.

God doesn't ask how many awards you
have won but asks how many people
you helped.
God doesn't ask how many hours you
prayed but asks how genuine your
prayers are.
God doesn't ask what you do in life but asks
how you live your life.

AUTHOR UNKNOWN

I Asked …
I asked for strength and God gave me
difficulties to make me strong.
I asked for wisdom and God gave me
problems to solve.
I asked for prosperity and God gave me
brawn and brains to work.
I asked for courage and God gave me
dangers to overcome.
I asked for patience and God placed me in
situations where I was forced to wait.

I asked for love and God gave me troubled
   people to help.
I asked for favours and God gave me
   opportunities.
I asked for everything so I could enjoy life.
Instead, He gave me life so I could enjoy
   everything.
I received nothing I wanted, I received
   everything I needed.

AUTHOR UNKNOWN

A Prayer from Africa

You asked for my hands
that you might use them for your purpose.
I gave them for a moment,
then withdrew them, for the work was hard.
You asked for my mouth
to speak out against injustice;
I gave you a whisper that I might not be
   accused.
You asked for my eyes

to see the pain of poverty;
I closed them, for I did not want to see.
You asked for my life
that you might work through me.
I gave a small part, that I might not get too
    involved.
Lord, forgive me for my calculated efforts to
    serve you
only when it is convenient for me to do so,
only in those places where it is safe to do so
and only with those who make it easy to
    do so.
Father, forgive me, renew me,
send me out as a usable instrument
that I might take seriously
the meaning of your cross.

ATTRIBUTED TO JOE SEREMANE

Life is

Life is an opportunity, benefit from it.

Life is beauty, admire it.

Life is a dream, realise it.

Life is a challenge, meet it.

Life is a duty, complete it.

Life is a game, play it.

Life is a promise, fulfil it.

Life is sorrow, overcome it.

Life is a song, sing it.

Life is a struggle, accept it.

Life is a tragedy, confront it.

Life is an adventure, dare it.

Life is luck, make it.

Life is too precious, do not destroy it.

Life is life, fight for it.

AUTHOR UNKNOWN

Pause and Pray

When in doubt, pause.

When tired, pause.

When angry, pause.

When stressed, pause.

And whenever you pause, pray.

AUTHOR UNKNOWN

I Believe

I believe in the sun even when it is not
shining.

I believe in love even when it is not around
me.

I believe in God even when God is silent.

INSCRIPTION ON A WALL
*of a cellar in Cologne, Germany, where a
number of Jews hid for the entire duration
of World War II*

Real Questions

Did I offer peace today?
Did I bring a smile to someone's face?
Did I say words of healing?
Did I let go of my anger and resentment?
Did I forgive?
Did I love?
These are real questions.

HENRI NOUWEN

Dear God

I know that I am not perfect,
I know sometimes I forget to pray
I know I have questioned my faith
I know sometimes I lose my temper
But thank you for loving me unconditionally
and giving me another day to start over
again.

AUTHOR UNKNOWN

Prayerful Reflection

Sometimes there are signs, and faith grows.
Other times no signs.
Signs of faith come simply as
the helping hand when times are rough,
the beauty of a flower which lifts the spirit,
the moment of peace in prayer,
the closeness of God in ritual,
the faith shared in community.
We can be amazed sometimes
at the ways we find faith strengthened.
Memories of family faith,
hymns sung that remind us of God,
and images filling the mind,
like our bodies being surrounded by light.
Jesus seems to expect that faith will be
   always here,
questioning yet hopeful,
that there will be times when only faith
   guides us,

and creates a trust that is strong but seems
    distant.
Always caring, our God,
even when it seems he sleeps.
Always the call, not to sleep
through others' tough moments.
And the openness to welcome and look for
    faith,
blowing like the wind, gently or loudly,
always a gift gratefully awaited and
    received.

DONAL NEARY

Called to Become

You are called to become
A perfect creation.
No one is called to become
Who you are called to be.
It does not matter
How short or tall
Or thick-set or slow
You may be.
It does not matter
Whether you sparkle with life
Or are as silent as a still pool.
Whether you sing your song aloud
Or weep alone in darkness.
It does not matter
Whether you feel loved and admired
Or unloved and alone
For you are called to become
A perfect creation.
No one's shadow
Should cloud your becoming.
No one's light
Should dispel your spark.

For the Lord delights in you.
Jealously looks upon you
And encourages with gentle joy
Every movement of the Spirit
Within you.
Unique and loved you stand,
Beautiful or stunted in your growth
But never without hope and life,
For you are called to become
A perfect creation.
This becoming may be
Gentle or harsh,
Subtle or violent,
But it never ceases.
Never pauses or hesitates.
Only is –
Creative force –
Calling you
Calling you to become
A perfect creation.

EDWINA GATELEY

Praying

It doesn't have to be
the blue iris, it could be
weeds in a vacant lot, or a few
small stones; just
pay attention, then patch

a few words together and don't try
to make them elaborate, this isn't
a contest but the doorway

into thanks, and a silence in which
another voice may speak.

MARY OLIVER

J.O.Y.

The key to finding joy is in the word itself.

J stands for Jesus
When we put Jesus at the centre of our lives everything else falls into place. If we follow the example of Jesus we will love one another.

O is for others
We can love others by sharing our time and talents with them. If we take time to appreciate everything that others do for us, our lives will be filled with gratitude.

Y is for yourself
Jesus said to love your neighbour as yourself. We have to take care of ourselves and love ourselves in order to be able to help others. We need to mind our physical,

mental and emotional health so that we can be the person that God created us to be.

If we remember to live our lives with this in mind then we will find joy.

AILÍS TRAVERS

Our Deepest Fear

Our deepest fear is not that we are inadequate. Our deepest fear is that we are powerful beyond measure. It is our light, not our darkness that most frightens us. We ask ourselves, Who am I to be brilliant, gorgeous, talented, fabulous? Actually, who are you not to be? You are a child of God. Your playing small does not serve the world. There is nothing enlightened about shrinking so that other people won't feel insecure around you. We are all meant to shine, as children do. We were born to make manifest the glory of God that is within us. It is not just in some of us; it is in everyone. And as we let our own light shine, we unconsciously give other people permission to do the same. As we are liberated from our own fear, our presence automatically liberates others.

MARIANNE WILLIAMSON

A Love Letter from God to His Children

My child I love you immensely with all my
    heart
Within your heart a beautiful garden grows
Bursting with sweet lilies and fragrant roses

You are a beautiful flower ready to grow
And blossom into who you are meant to be
I have painted every flower with a beautiful
    hue
And your life with a beautiful purpose

Dearest, you are unique, you are beautiful
Remember that always

Keep those words engraved in your heart
And know that you are never alone
I have engraved your name in the palm of
my hand

You are precious in my eyes
I love you with an everlasting love

Do not be afraid
I am with you always until the end of time
Do not worry about what might be
Or what could be, but focus on what is, the
present

All my love
Your heavenly Father.

The Optimist Creed
Promise Yourself
To be so strong that nothing
can disturb your peace of mind.
To talk health, happiness, and prosperity
to every person you meet.

To make all your friends feel
that there is something in them.
To look at the sunny side of everything
and make your optimism come true.

To think only the best, to work only for the
best, and to expect only the best.
To be just as enthusiastic about the success
of others as you are about your own.

To forget the mistakes of the past
and press on to the greater achievements
of the future.

To wear a cheerful countenance at all times
and give every living creature you meet a
smile.

To give so much time to the improvement
of yourself
that you have no time to criticise others.
To be too large for worry, too noble for
anger, too strong for fear,
and too happy to permit the presence of
trouble.

To think well of yourself and to proclaim this
fact to the world,
not in loud words but great deeds.
To live in faith that the whole world is on
your side,
so long as you are true to the best that is in
you.

CHRISTIAN D. LARSON

Be Still
and
know that
I am

GOD

PSALM 46:10

MEDITATIONS

If someone asked you to use another word for 'God', you could use the word 'Presence', for that is what God is. A presence that is always with us. It has been said that God is as close as our own breath. Therefore, when we pray we are simply becoming aware of a presence that is always there. We do not need any words to be aware of this presence. In fact, if we just spend some time in silence we are more likely to be aware of God's presence with us. Try the following short meditation exercises to begin a time of stillness and silence.

Body Exercise

Sit in your chair, upright but comfortable, with your back supported. Let your body relax (without slouching), with your feet on the floor in front of you and your hands at rest on your thighs or joined in your lap.

Close your eyes, or fix them on some point in front of you. Now let your whole attention focus on what you can feel in your body. You may start at your feet and work upwards, letting your attention dwell, perhaps only for a few seconds, on whatever part of the body you can feel, shifting attention from one part of the body to the other, although the longer you can hold attention on one part, the better.

Your attention is on what you are feeling, not on thoughts about feeling. If you are uncomfortable, or itchy or want to move position, just acknowledge the discomfort, assure yourself that it is all right and, without moving, continue to focus attention on what you can feel in the body.

ADAPTED FROM GERRY W. HUGHES SJ
God of Surprises

Breathing Exercise
This exercise involves concentrating all your attention on the physical feelings of breathing in and breathing out, without deliberately changing the rhythm of your breathing.

Focus attention on feeling the cold air entering your nostrils and the warm air when you exhale. At first you may become self-conscious about your breathing and find it becomes irregular, but this does not, as a rule, continue. If it were to do so, and you find yourself becoming breathless, then this exercise is not for you at present. Most people find that on doing this exercise, the pattern of their breathing changes, the breath becoming deeper and slower, and they begin to feel drowsy. In itself, it is a very good relaxation exercise, but if you care to use it for more explicit prayer, then let the in-breathing express all that you long for in life, however impossible it may seem in practice, and let the out-breath express your surrender of everything to God, all of your life with its worries, sins, guilt and regrets.

It is important to do this without self-judgement, whether of approval or disapproval. Keep your attention fixed on your desire to hand over all these worries about self, and do not clutch at them as if they were a treasured possession.

ADAPTED FROM GERRY W. HUGHES SJ
God of Surprises

Listening Exercise

Sit in your chair, upright but comfortable, with your back supported.

Now just notice the sounds that you can hear, sounds far away.

Just hear them, don't even try to name them …

Notice fainter sounds, then sounds which are nearer.

Just listen, become aware of them …

And the sound of your own heartbeat, faint, but your own rhythm of life …

And the sound of silence in your place of prayer, the silence within yourself …

Listen like this for a few minutes.

ADAPTED FROM DONAL NEARY SJ
Praying in Lent

Personal Notes

God speaks in the silence
of the heart. Listening is the
beginning of Prayer

— Blessed Mother Teresa

J̲ esus
O̲ thers
Y̲ ourself

When life gives you more than you can stand . . .
Kneel!

When you can't put your prayers into words, God hears your heart

A + S + A + P
ALWAYS STOP AND PRAY

God has three answers
to your prayers:
YES · NOT YET
I HAVE SOMETHING BETTER
IN MIND

PRAYER: The world's greatest wireless connection.

F̲ orwarding
A̲ ll
I̲ ssues
T̲ o
H̲ eaven

Pray always,
Pray all ways

Why wish upon a star when you can pray to the one who created it!

185

Suggested Scripture Passages for
Lectio divina

1 John 4:7-11
God is Love

Mark 4:35-41
Jesus Stills a Storm

Matthew 5:1-12
The Beatitudes

Matthew 5:13-16
Salt and Light

Luke 2:41-52
The Boy Jesus in the Temple

Romans 12:9-21
Marks of the True Christian

Psalm 23
The Divine Shepherd

Luke 1:26-38
The Annunciation to Mary

Luke 2:1-20
The Birth of Jesus

Luke 22:19-20
Jesus Institutes the Holy Eucharist on Holy Thursday

Luke 22:39-65
Jesus' Agony in the Garden and Arrest

Luke 23:33-56
The Crucifixion and Death of Christ

John 20:11-18
Jesus Appears to Mary Magdalene after the Resurrection

Acts 2:1-4
Pentecost: Public Manifestation of the Church

Acknowledgements

Grateful acknowledgement is made to the following holders of copyright material:

All scripture quotations, except on p. 108, taken from the *New Revised Standard Version Holy Bible* © 1989, 1995 Division of Christian Education of the National Council of the Churches of Christ in the United States of America. All rights reserved.

Scripture quotation on p. 108, taken from *New King James Version* © 1982 Thomas Nelson, Inc. All rights reserved.

All papal quotes © Libreria Editrice Vaticana. Used with permission.

'Pray with Scripture', pp. 16–18, adapted from the Catholic Schools Week 2012 guide to *Lectio divina*. Copyright © 2012 Catholic Schools Partnership.

All prayers by Orla Walsh taken from *FaithConnect*, Veritas Publications. Copyright © 2011 Orla Walsh. Used with permission.

'Today is My Day', pp. 27–8, by Dr Barbara L. King. Copyright © Dr Barbara L. King. Used with permission.

Every effort has been made to contact the copyright holders of the material reproduced in *Oxygen for the Soul: Prayers, Reflections and Inspiration for Teenagers*. If any infringement of copyright has occurred, the owners of such copyright are requested to contact the publishers.

heartchildren.ie/blue-ribbon-fund

All Terrain Pushair Walks Brecon Beacons

Published by Sigma Leisure – an imprint of
Sigma Press, Stobart House, Pontyclerc, Penybanc Road, Ammanford, Carmarthenshire SA18 3HP.

British Library Cataloguing in Publication Data
A CIP record for this book is available from the British Library.

ISBN: 978-1-85058-909-9

Typesetting and Design by: Sigma Press, Ammanford.

Cover photograph: © Simon Johnson

Maps and photographs: © Simon Johnson

Symbols: Rebecca Chippindale and Rebecca Terry

Printed by: TJ International Ltd, Padstow, Cornwall

Disclaimer: the information in this book is given in good faith and is believed to be correct at the time of publication. No responsibility is accepted by either the author or publisher for errors or omissions, or for any loss or injury howsoever caused. Only you can judge your own fitness, competence and experience. Do not reply soley on sketch mas for nagivations: we strongly recommend the use of appropriate Ordnance Survey (or equivalent) maps.

All Terrain Pushair
Walks Brecon Beacons

Simon and Rebecca Johnson

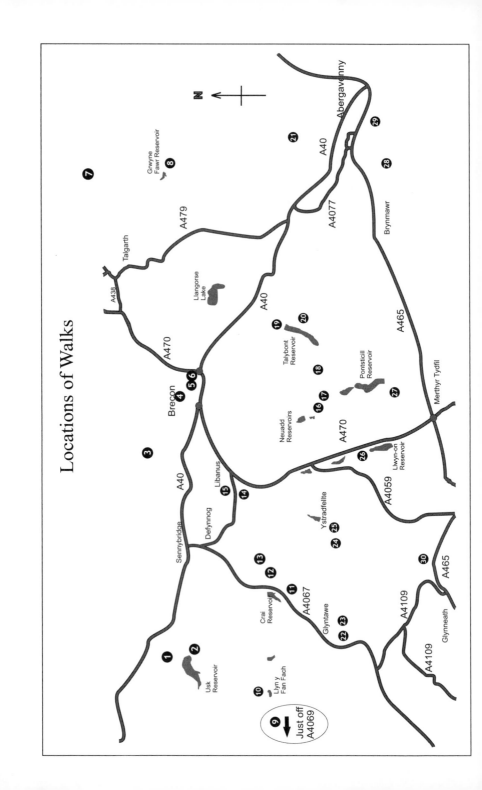

Locations of Walks

Contents

Dedicated to our five long-suffering children, Catrin, Anna, Rhiannon, Harri and William, who have been on so many walks with us, urged on when feeling despondent with the phrase – "Come on, it's for the book!" Here is your little bit of fame: Catrin our intrepid explorer, Anna who is always in need of snacks, Rhiannon who falls in lakes and cowpats, Harri who walks but mainly runs the distance, and William the baby who wants to get in and out of the ATP when it suits him! Well done, you have been little troopers. We have so many memories which will be treasured for years.

Key to symbols

 Easy walk

 Moderate walk

 Strenuous walk

 Circular route

 There-and-back

 Trainers suitable

 Walking boots essential

 Achievable solo

 Two people needed

 Suitable for double ATPs

 Stile/obstacle

WC Toilets

 Tea shop

 Picnic area

 Pub

 Ducks

 Ice cream van/shop

 Playground

8

Introduction

This book is written for families wanting to take their children walking using All Terrain Pushchairs (ATPs) on beautiful walks in the Brecon Beacons National Park. The walks are also suitable for families without ATPs and anyone wishing to enjoy a walk without too much gradient and few if any, stiles. The paths are suitable for double ATPs, as we have walked them all with our own double ATP. Most routes have been walked twice, some many times. The routes have all been carefully researched and planned.

Simon and Rebecca Johnson have both grown up with a love of the countryside and walking. Simon was raised on a farm in Herefordshire and quickly developed a passion for the outdoors. Rebecca was brought up in the Welsh valleys and her love for walking came through many family holidays to the Lake District. Both are teachers, although Rebecca left teaching after the birth of their first child to become a full-time mother. They mainly take their five children walking and cycling in the Brecon Beacons, the Lake District and Scotland.

Hopefully there will be outdoor and walking tips to be found within the book, gained through our experience of parenting, although we would both be the first to admit that we are still learning!

There are route maps which accompany each walk, to make it easier to understand the intended route. It is advisable to use an Ordnance Survey map in conjunction with this book, and to be able to use a compass and know how to use a grid reference. The routes have timings attached to them, although these are quite approximate and depend upon how many times you stop for drinks, snacks, changing clothing or nappies, tying laces etc? (I have recently taken to tying triple knots, as it is no joke when presented with eight laces that have come untied!) At what speed do you walk? How fit are you and your children? What takes us two hours with our five, will often take other families just over an hour – see the earlier note on shoe laces! However, most people will find it easy to gauge the walk from the distance, difficulty rating and the amount of ascent (how much height you will have gained by the end of the walk).

The Brecon Beacons provides an excellent source of beauty, wildlife and tranquillity. Whilst some parts of the Central Beacons are extremely popular and frequented by many a walker, other lesser known parts are much quieter, yet wild and unspoilt. Bringing up children to enjoy walking and appreciate the fun of the mountain environment, will more often than not instil a love for the outdoors in them, and improve their fitness! Active children eat well and sleep better at night. Walking is a free day out. Hopefully this book will introduce you to some of Wales' best kept secrets.

Get the most out of walking with your children

Mountain Air is Fresher!
Walking is a pleasure that combines exercise with fresh air, beautiful scenery and wildlife. It is also easy on the wallet, with few if any charges. For many, when going to a mountainous area for a holiday it makes sense to pick up a book with a list of routes ready to walk, rather than spend half the holiday pouring over a map looking for suitable routes. Having a book like this should give confidence and provide reassurance that the paths outlined in the book are suitable for ATPs, knowing that the routes have all been tried and tested by ourselves with our children during various seasons. Generally more than once, sometimes frequently!

Know your children
Having a love for the great outdoors should naturally rub off on your children, and with a bit of luck, your passion for walking will be adopted by them. I remember taking our children on a fairly difficult walk, and when our eldest daughter started complaining, realised that I had overestimated her ability on the difficult terrain, and turned back. At other times, we have motivated them to continue, using distraction techniques – singing, looking for wildlife, promise of treats, anything. We have provided them with nappy sacks to collect pine cones, leaves and pebbles which is a great distraction! Knowing your children's abilities and limitations is something you learn as a parent. Family walks should, ultimately, be a pleasure, not a chore. Children should look forward to them, not dread them!

Hints and Tips (including advice for those already walking)

All Terrain Pushchair
Little advice needs to be given on this subject, as most parents know what they want. Some useful features to look out for include:
  • Select the most lightweight model that you can afford – it's very different pushing a heavily laden ATP up a mountain than it is around town

- Having a fixed wheel, or a lockable swivel wheel when encountering very rough terrain – otherwise a non-lockable swivel wheel will get stuck on more uneven ground
- Easily removable wheels make for easy packing in the back of the vehicle (carrier bags are useful when wheels can't be cleaned at the end of a walk!)
- Filling the tyres with anti-puncture slime sealant is fantastic for avoiding punctures. Even the most benign looking thorn can cause a puncture without it
- Bent valves make for much easier tyre inflation than those that aren't
- Make sure that you keep a pump and puncture repair kit on the ATP
- Storage – the more storage your ATP can offer, the better. You can even buy extra storage slings that fit under the current sling. This is a bit of a trade-off with the clearance height that the ATP will lose
- A large and effective sun shade, rain cover and foot muff
- An ATP that collapses easily (try it in the shop!) and is compact
- A hand operated brake is useful for steep descents, as is a wrist strap (which should be worn on descents!)
- A warm foot muff may be needed all year round; the wind at higher altitudes can make it very chilly even in high summer. Extra blankets are essential in colder seasons.

A toy on a strap can help to keep a baby entertained. Making sure your toy and soother are on straps can save many stops to retrieve the invariably dirty item! Newborns should not be taken over rocky ground before they are three months old. If you do take a younger baby (three months and older), a newborn head support insert is a good idea (or roll a blanket into a 'sausage' around the head).

Rain, wind and sun protection
A good quality foot muff that comes up quite high on the child will ensure warmth. Exposed hills will often be cold, even in summer. Always carry a spare blanket to wrap around the baby when removing him/her from the pushchair to feed or change. The rain cover makes an excellent wind shield. It should remembered, however, that in effect you have created a greenhouse and you should monitor their temperature. We have found that with two children under a rain cover,

it soon gets hot and airless inside the ATP, and some of the children's layers may need to be removed, as well as unzipping foot muffs in order to avoid over heating. Rebecca discovered this on a wet summer walk in the Lake District. She put her head inside the rain cover to attend to the baby, and found it quite unbearable. We quickly lifted the raincover to allow cool, fresh air to circulate. This was a lesson quickly learnt. Don't assume that all is well just because the baby is fast asleep.

A large sun canopy is vital. A parasol will more than likely prove to be more of a hindrance in the wind; a blanket and clothes pegs are quite effective as are the all-round UV shades which are now available. Making sure children have sun cream on before going for a walk is important in the summer months. Children need to drink regularly, and we always take additional water with us – enough for cleaning cuts or washing the apple that has been dropped etc! It is always best to have too much that is not needed. Children will be miserable if affected by dehydration. Sun hats and sun glasses are useful if your baby complies! Remember that babies and children become dehydrated far more quickly than adults.

Clothing

If your children are in the ATP for prolonged periods of time, their body temperature will be lower than yours as they enjoy the ride. Their body temperature will fall further when they sleep. Children should have lots of layers during colder periods – layers can be altered to suit the temperature. Waterproof jackets can be added to stop the wind. No matter how sunny it looks outside, even if the sun is blazing and there are no clouds in the sky, remember the weather in the mountain environment can change rapidly. Always err on the side of caution and take waterproof jackets, and some warm clothing. It is always best to have too much than too little. Spare clothing should be packed in plastic bags in your rucksack (don't forget spare socks and underwear for children who are attracted to deep muddy puddles!). Fleece hats and even gloves are a useful and light accessory even in the middle of the Summer (as we discovered in a Lake District summer). As mentioned briefly before, splashsuits are excellent and keep children relatively warm and dry (obviously with layers underneath). Keep away from denim as it does not dry out if your child gets wet. Go for quicker drying materials (such as fleece – they don't have to be expensive outdoor makes). These are becoming more readily available in a wider range of sizes from outdoor shops and online. If your child falls over in a stream, or whilst paddling in a lake, they are more likely to dry out if wearing quick drying clothing. Again, we realised the importance of quick drying clothing after our third daughter, Rhiannon, tested a branch over Buttermere during our summer holiday and took an unexpected dip in the lake!

Footwear
Walking boots tend to me more sensible as your children get older, and routes get a little longer. Wellies are great for muddy and shorter routes, although they may rub, and can be sweaty in the summer and cold in the winter. Take care walking in the snow with wellies - keep walks brief as your child's feet may become very cold. They certainly have their place, nonetheless. Trainers are great when the trail is dry.

Map and Compass
Little navigation is needed on most of these walks, although it really cannot be emphasised enough how important it is to understand and be able to use an Ordnance Survey map, and ideally a compass as well. I always take my map and compass with me. A GPS will provide you with a grid reference should you need to know exactly where you are on the map. Although not essential, many phones are now equipped with GPSs and are able to download Ordnance Survey maps. These can be an excellent navigational backup aid.

Food, baby feeding and nappies
Children love to have a picnic, and we often take a picnic with us that we eat along the route. We always take plenty of food, and let our children snack on fruit - dried or fresh - whilst we are walking to keep up energy. As mentioned we often take treats, particularly if the walk is a bit longer. Chocolate is an excellent motivational tool, and gives a useful energy burst. I keep some high energy sweets/gels as a back up. Wipes and alcohol gel are both useful for hygiene, especially when eating on the go! A collapsible travel potty is useful for a child of that age, and disposable nappies are preferable to the washable sort when out walking (they are absorbent for longer, have fewer leaks, are more compact to carry when soiled and easier to change in an awkward place). A baby can easily be changed inside the footmuff on a cold day but should ideally be done in the car whenever possible. In warmer weather, use your lap, or expensive jacket as a changing mat! Breast

feeding is very easy and hygenic when out and about and will warm up your baby if for any reason he/she has lost heat. Likewise, in warm weather it provides all the hydration your baby needs. Bottle fed babies can easily be catered for by heating the water to a warmer temperature than is needed beforehand and carrying in a well-insulated bottle bag. Simply add the powdered formula milk when needed. This will ensure the milk doesn't go off. Alternatively, if your child doesn't object, cartons of ready made formula milk are very useful. Remember to take additional water in warm weather for bottle fed babies.

Survival kit
You may think it a little over the top to think of a survival kit when taking your children on a short walk, but accidents can happen. We always take a foil thermal blanket, mobile phone, money, first aid kit, and chocolate. A bottle of antihistamine medicine (appropriate to the child's age) is also useful should you encounter stinging nettles, heat rash or insect bites or stings in the hills. Remember many of these cause drowsiness, so ask your pharmacist for one which does not.

Motivating your children to walk
(They won't be in the ATP all their lives!)

Choose fun routes
Our children's favourite walk is actually a very steep walk up Cribarth (the 'Sleeping Giant', Abercraf) with a height ascent of 300m (although we don't always go to the very top). They love the variety – lots of stiles to climb (not ATP suitable!), plenty of woodland to walk through, lots of wildlife to see, a ruined farm house, the 'dinosaur tree', a huge boulder to climb on, etc. Variety is the spice of life!

Play the Teacher
Talk to your children as you are walking. Give them science and geography lessons. Point out things of interest. Give them small bags to collect acorns, leaves, pine cones, etc. These can be painted or glued to make a collage at home for a rainy day activity.

Buying gear
Some people who enjoy walking are sometimes accused of being 'gear freaks'. They walk with a vast array of gadgets and gear. For children

though, the odd item of gear adds interest and motivation. Simple cheap compasses, binoculars, skipping ropes (great for towing each other, playing horses, etc), junior walking poles, and walky talkies are all fun and provide fun during the walk – possibly even distracting when they are a little tired. Packing your child's own little rucksack is great fun for them. An older child might want to carry his or her own camera.

Treats
Healthy snacks are a good idea for little ones in order to maintain their sugar levels. Some treats for the walk are always helpful. Whilst fruit and dried fruit is best, and can be nibbled on regularly during the walk, a little chocolate, as mentioned earlier, is a great motivator!

Geocaching
Imagine being pirates for a day, hunting for buried treasure! This is geocaching. If you are not aware of it, there are containers hidden around various parts of Britain. You download the grid reference onto your GPS, and then locate the treasure. When you eventually find the stash, you take a gift from it – colouring pencils, key ring, etc, and put something back in its place.

Walking in the Brecon Beacons
Unfortunately, the Brecon Beacons are not quite as open as some other national parks such as the Lake District. What we mean by this is that there is an abundance of stiles, locked gates and kissing gates. Whether to keep out off-road motor cyclists or for some other reason, although they do not affect the walker, they most certainly do affect the ATP walker. They have repeatedly frustrated us on what would have been otherwise excellent walks. The walks in this book try to avoid them as much as possible, although on some walks, they are unavoidable.

I hope you haven't been put off walking altogether! As parents you will of course, use your own common sense and judgement as to how much kit you carry, we merely seek to share our experience of what we find useful. Once it is all packed, many of these things can stay under the ATP, or ready packed in a rucksack. Get your children into the fresh air and enjoy yourselves!

Walk 1
Mynydd Bach Trecastell – Roman Fort

If you enjoy history along with fantastic views of the length of the Brecon Beacons, this could be a very enjoyable walk for you. The walk follows the old Roman road and there are the remains of two Roman marching camps, two stone circles (three if you include one just off the metalled road), a small Norman motte, and the sites of 'hafod' (summer dwellings) of the Iron Age. There are also a number of wild ponies roaming which can often be spotted. This is red kite country, and worth keeping a look out for them. You will also hear tank firing from the Epynt firing ranges on some days. The track is a well used

Distance	2.9 miles (4.6km) or if the final section is walked: 4.4 miles (7km)
Ascent	145ft (44m) or if the final section is walked: 210ft (64m)
Allow	Shorter route: 2 hours; Longer route: 3-4 hours
Terrain	Well worn grassy track with deep ruts, some long puddles
Map	OS Explorer Map OL12 / Landranger Map 160. Grid ref SN 845 300
Amenities	Public toilets in Sennybridge. Very useful and well stocked Londis Shop shortly after Sennybridge. Turning off the A40, take the signs for the Usk Reservoir, there is a park by the Antique Centre

grassy track, with fairly deep ruts along most of its length. In wet weather, these ruts fill with water and are a nuisance, although it is often possible to walk round them. The walk can be lengthened by going off the beaten track to the trig point at Comen y Rhos.

Directions to starting point

Driving west along the A40, take the next turning left after the turning for the Usk Reservoir. The turn off is next to the 'Antique Centre'. Follow the road upwards, and take the first turn right in about half a mile. The road follows the course of the old Roman road and as you can imagine is fairly straight. The road comes to an end at a gate with the sign 'unsuitable for motor vehicles.' This is the start of the walk.

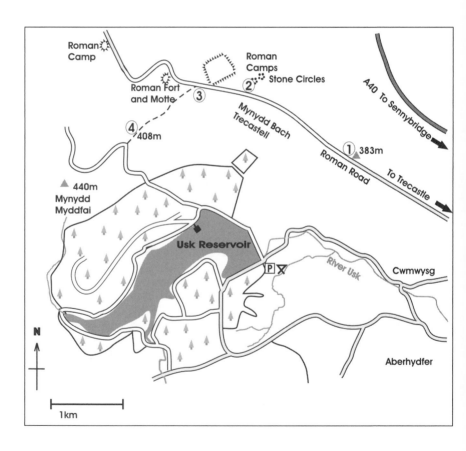

The Route

1. From the gate follow the track.

2. After about 1 mile, the track has a number of large boulders running along side it. Clearly visible are some fairly deep and long puddles. This is a sensible place to turn back, following the same route.

3. **For the very adventurous**
It is possible to take a lesser worn track that cuts left immediately before the stone boulders on the side of the main track. The grassy path makes its way across some fairly testing and upwardly inclined terrain towards the trig point at Comen y Rhos.

4. It is unlikely that you will get that far, although you might make it to the top of the grassy knoll at 408m. The views may make up for the hard slog!

Looking across the Usk Reservoir with the Carmarthen Fan in the background

Walk 2
Usk Reservoir

The Usk reservoir is a large, beautiful, upland reservoir, at a height of just over 1,000 feet. It is in a remote corner of the Brecon Beacons, surrounded by forestry and offers excellent views of the Carmarthen Fan (Bannau Sir Gaer). It has plenty of wildlife, including red kites. Fishing is available between March and October, with day tickets available from the self-service ticket dispenser on site. The path itself is used by mountain bikes and circles the whole lake, with a small but ankle deep ford crossing to be made half way round.

Distance	5.3 miles (8.6km) – (half way) or 5.2 miles (8.4km) – (circular)
Ascent	460ft (136m) – (half way) or 562ft (171m) – (circular)
Allow	3-4 hours
Terrain	Tarmac and excellent gravel paths with little gradient to the half way point. The path becomes muddy and steep at times after the half way point if doing the circular walk
Map	OS Explorer Map OL12 / Landranger Map 160. Grid ref SN 833 286
Amenities	Public toilets in Sennybridge. Very useful and well stocked Londis Shop shortly after Sennybridge. Turning off the A40, taking the signs for the Usk Reservoir, there is a park by the Antique Centre

Looking across the tranquil Usk Reservoir

It is up to you, whether you do a full circular of the reservoir, or walk part of the way round it, and then return via the same route (this is one of the longer walks). The circular route is not quite as appealing as it first sounds. The track deteriorates to some extent after crossing the small ford and becomes steep and muddy for a short section. In addition, views on the other side of the reservoir are far more limited for most of the walk. However, there is something interesting about not having to return via the same route.

Directions to starting point

From the east (Brecon direction), take the A40 through Sennybridge and on to Trecastle. The Usk reservoir is signposted left. Take the turning at the Castle Coaching Inn. After about half a mile you will go over a bridge. Continue straight, signposted Pont ar Hydfer & Cwmwysg. You will see a right turn again signposted 'Usk Reservoir' after about 3 miles. Follow this road and park by the head of the dam

The Route

The route is best taken in an anti-clockwise direction, as the path hugs the north shores of the reservoir affording lovely views. The path on the north side is excellent, starting as tarmac and turning into a smooth forestry commission track. The tracks on the south side are good, but muddy and steep at times and with fewer views of the reservoir. The walk can be completed as a circular walk if there are two adults for pushing, or walking to the ford and back makes a good alternative if wanting to use better paths and enjoy more pleasant views.

1. The path around the reservoir is marked by mountain bike symbols. From the car park, cross the dam wall (your ATP should just squeeze under the gate if you tilt it back). Follow the tarmac roadway around the edge of the reservoir. You will get the best views along this section of the roadway.

2. The roadway comes to an end by the Tower in the reservoir (this is also the last picnic bench). Take the forest track that branches off

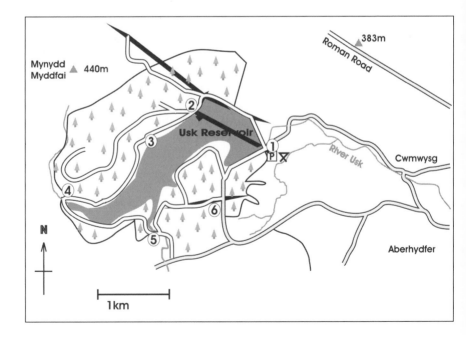

to the right, heading upwards. There is a gate across the track (which again the ATP should just squeeze under). The track then splits in two. Take the left track.

3. The track runs past some grassy knolls, ideal if picnicking has not already taken place. At the end of the 'leg of the reservoir' the path crosses a ford. For many people, this will be a good place to turn around and retrace your steps.

4. For the adventurous, the ford is manageable, although a wet foot is a strong possibility! There are some stepping stones by the ford. The path soon becomes a little muddy, and within a short time, there is a steep section. At the end of the steep section, the path is much drier, and there are some views of the Carmarthen Fans (Bannau Sir Gaer) again. The track drops down and crosses a river (courtesy of a bridge) this time.

5. The track then divides into two. Take the left fork (the right fork takes you to the road). The track then climbs, becomes a little muddy again. It then meets the road.

6. Turn left onto the road which will take you back to the car park.

Walk 3
Aberbran

This walk is a quiet, pleasant countryside walk through common land that takes you along a ridge high above Aberbran with fine views in most directions, including across the Beacons. There are often horses and sheep about which make life a little more interesting for little ones. As you leave Aberbran you will notice a beautifully maintained bench on the side of the road with lovely views. A more ideal picnicking spot will not be found!

Directions to starting point
From the A40 heading west from Brecon, take the turning to Aberbran. Follow the road for a short distance and at the junction, turn right (signposted Cradoc, Aberyscir, & Llanfihangel Nant Bran). You will

Distance	1.9 miles (3.1km)
Ascent	208ft (63m)
Allow	1-1½ hours
Terrain	Excellent grassy tracks with very little gradient. Muddy at certain times of the year. There is one slightly testing short uphill section
Map	OS Explorer Map OL12 / Landranger Map 160. Grid ref SN 986 325
Amenities	None in the locality, although there are toilets in the lay-by between Brecon and Aberbran on the A40

soon come to the village of Aberyscir, and on leaving the village will come across a very narrow stone bridge. Turn left immediately before the bridge. After about half a mile, the road forks, take the left fork. The road climbs and after passing over a cattle grid, the road opens up as you reach the common. The walk starts from the first footpath sign that you see on the left (quite overgrown). Stop here. If you reach a sign for a bridleway, you have gone too far, although you could walk from here, as the bridleway links up with the described path (although it may be more muddy). Parking is available on the common, or wherever can be found on the side of the road.

The Route

1. From the sign, you will see that there are three paths. Take the middle, less distinct track which heads for the centre of two trees

Easy paths amongst the secluded common land

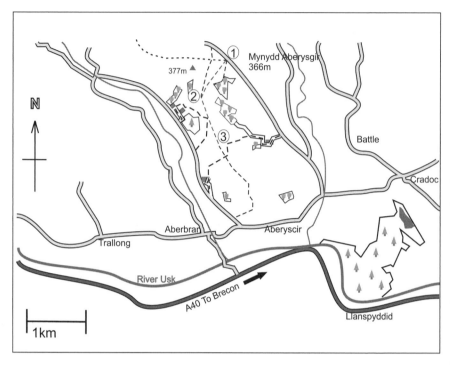

and the edge of the field. The track then follows the boundary fence of two fields, with oak trees overhanging the second field.

2. Soon after, the track starts to bear to the left and the strip of land between the two fields become quite narrow. The path splits – take the left hand track (which saves unnecessary climbing). The two paths converge then divide. Take the one on the right that heads uphill quite steeply between gorse bushes. Stay on this path, going between more gorse, ignoring the track that branches to the left at the top of the climb.

3. Stay on this track which stays close to the stone wall on the right and eventually comes to a very climbable oak tree! Return along the same path.

Walk 4
Pen y Crug

A convenient gem of a walk from Brecon. Pen y Crug is a fascinating Iron Age hill-fort. It is a large and very impressive site. Being on a prominent and fairly steep hill, it was clearly easy to defend. There are a series of ramparts around the summit of the hill, as well as a fantastic 360 degree view. The walk is short, and can be completed quite quickly, although it should be noted that it is quite steep for two short sections, and the path is narrow again for a short section, with brambles on either side of the path. However, the effort is rewarded with stunning views of the Breconshire countryside and the Brecon

Distance	2 miles (3.2km)
Ascent	477ft (145m)
Allow	1½ hours
Terrain	A decent path for most of the walk, although there are two short steep sections, and one short narrow section (manageable with a double ATP, but with brambles – so puncture resistant sludge is useful). The last pull up to the fort is also quite steep
Map	OS Explorer Map OL12 / Landranger Map 160. Grid ref SO 042 296
Amenities	There is parking available at the start of the walk and around Brecon. There are toilets, shops and places to eat in Brecon's historic town

Beacons and is an ideal walk from the centre of Brecon. The ramparts make the walk that bit more exciting for the children.

Directions to starting point

From Brecon, take the B4520 (sign-posted Upper Chapel), going past Brecon Cathedral. Go up through Pendre, and the start of the walk is the bridleway marked on the left immediately after Maes-y-Ffynnon Road. The bridleway is at the end of the built up area. If driving, and you find yourself in countryside with Lower Pontgwilym Farm on your right, you have gone past the turning.

The Route

1. From the start of the bridleway, the path starts off as tarmac quickly turning stony and takes a sharp turn to the left (marked by a signpost) by a wooden gate.

A short walk from Brecon enjoying gorgeous views and a chance to play around the summit

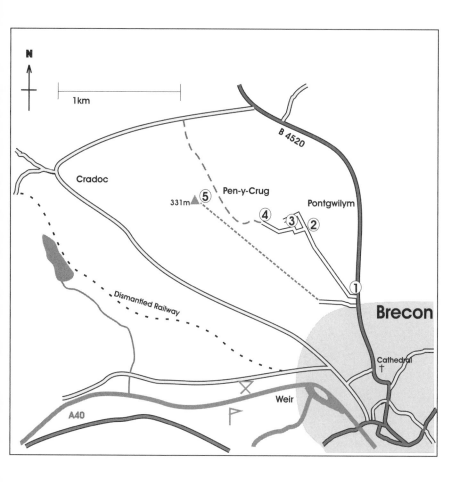

2. The track becomes a little steeper, although quite manageable. It then steepens quite significantly as it turns to concrete. The concrete track ends by a house, and the track reduces in width and quality.

3. The brambles can prove a nuisance, and after 50 yards the track turns left and becomes much more narrow and steep. It is passable even for a double ATP, although again beware of the brambles puncturing the tyres (if you don't use puncture resistant slime). Fortunately the path only lasts for about 50 yards before a wooden gate is reached.

4. The gate marks the open heath. Go through the gate and follow the sign post. The white trig point is visible and marks the end of the walk. The path is now grass, and although short is again steep. The fort is not really visible until you are upon it. The views are outstanding, and there is a 360 degree viewfinder on the top of the trig point.

5. The return is simply a reversal of the route.

Walk 5
Brecon River Usk

This is a very easy, flat walk alongside the River Usk. For much of the route, the path is of tarmac, with benches, and a children's play park. The tarmac ends by the football pitch where you walk through a meadow. It is a tranquil walk with possibilities for children to play in the park, as well as picnic enjoying views of Pen y Fan across the river.

Directions to starting point

From the main river bridge in Brecon, stay on the Brecon side of the river, and follow the road that heads north-west alongside the river.

Distance	**1.6 miles (2.6km)**
Ascent	**64ft (20m)**
Allow	**1 hour**
Terrain	**A flat, easy walk mainly on tarmac, though with some grass at the end**
Map	**OS Explorer Map OL12 / Landranger Map 160. Grid ref SO 042 286**
Amenities	**There are toilets in Brecon, and some along the walk (at the Upper Meadow car park next to the football pitch on the promenade) as well as numerous places to park your vehicle. Along the walk, there is a children's play park, as well as boat hire and a basic café in the Promenade car park (open from late spring to the autumn)**

It crosses a tributary of the Usk (the Honddu), and within a very short time, you will see a foot bridge (which is the start of the walk) that takes you to the River Usk.

The Route

1. At the start of the walk, there is a signpost showing 'To the Boat House'. Walk over the little bridge to pick up the path that goes alongside the river. You will notice that there are plenty of benches along its length.

2. Continue along the path past the weir until you come to the Boat House. Take the path to the left that leads down past the Boat House.

3. Soon after, you will see a children's play park on the right, and the path continues through a meadow.

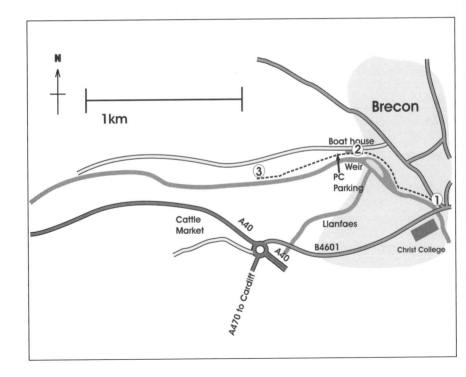

An easy and convenient walk from Brecon

4. At the end of the meadow, there is a narrow kissing gate, which is where you need to turn around and follow the river back to the start.

Walk 6
Brecon Canal

This walk is an ideal walk from the centre of Brecon, and is an easy walk as it is flat. Ducks will often be seen on the canal, as well as canal boats, which of course provide interest for the younger walker. About half a mile down the canal path, there is a life sized model of a horse and tram, explaining a little of the local history. It might be an idea to take some food to feed the ducks!

Directions to starting point
From the middle of Brecon, take the signs for the theatre and the canal. The theatre is located at the start of the canal.

Distance	Up to 35 miles – it's up to you
Ascent	Flat, it's a canal!
Allow	30 minutes to as long as you want
Terrain	A wide, popular and well used canal path
Map	OS Explorer Map OL12 / Landranger Map 160. Grid ref SO 046 282
Amenities	There are toilets a short way down the canal walk. There are also toilets and shops in Brecon

The start of the canal makes a beautiful setting next to the theatre

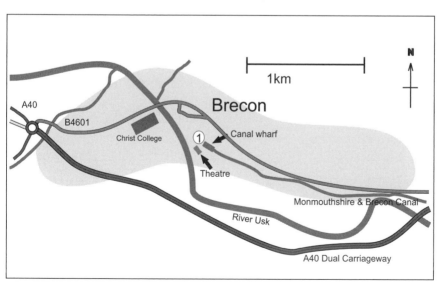

The Route

1. Walk down the right hand side of the canal, as the left hand side stops abruptly in a few yards. About half a mile or so down the path, you will come across a model of a horse and tram which younger walkers will find interesting. It is entirely up to you how far you walk. Return via the same route.

Walk 7
Hay Bluff

Hay Bluff is a popular, quaint tourist spot eight minutes from the picturesque town of Hay-on-Wye, famed for its numerous second hand books and shops. The Gospel Pass road starts from Hay-on-Wye and Capel-y-Ffin and climbs to an impressive 542m between Hay Bluff and Lord Hereford's Knob. Hay Bluff is a favourite launch point for hang-gliders and offers incomparable views over the Wye Valley and far into central Wales. There are lovely views from the start of the walk, and on a sunny day is a great place for a picnic. The walk skirts the front of Hay Bluff, and provides some easy walking with a couple of short, rough sections due to tractor tyres.

Distance	1.9 miles (3km)
Ascent	271ft (82m)
Allow	1 hour
Terrain	Good grassy paths, with a couple of muddy sections churned up by tractors. Very slight incline/gradient
Map	Explorer Map OL13 / Landranger Map 161. SO 239 373
Amenities	Shops and toilets in the popular tourist town of Hay-on-Wye

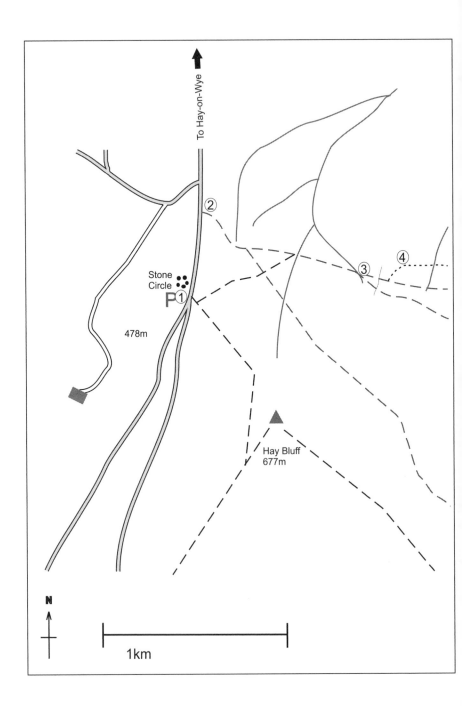

To Hay-on-Wye

②

Stone
Circle

P①

478m

③ ④

▲
Hay Bluff
677m

N

1km

Directions to starting point

From Hay-on-Wye, take the road marked Capel-y-Ffin. The road is later signposted the Gospel Pass. The road climbs for some time, and when it starts to level out, you will see a car park on the right just before a junction. This is the starting point of the walk.

The Route

1. From the car park next to the stone circle, walk back down the road about 300m until you see a sign for the Offa's Dyke Path on the right hand side. Take this path. As you start from the road, you will see a lobe heading towards the bottom of Hay Bluff. On the lobe, two tracks can be seen climbing it. One heading towards the hill, and one away from it. This is the one you are heading towards. Cross a small stream and take the steeper track as the left hand one is impassable.

The lovely view from the Hay-Bluff car park

2. The bridleway clearly splits with the one path heading up towards Hay Bluff (which you saw at the start of the walk). Take the left hand path.

3. The path forks again. Take the left path as the right hand path is impassable.

4 Cross a tiny stream and continue straight over a couple of flat stones where the bridleway forks to the right. Stay on the broader track which sweeps round to the right.

5. As the path nears the field's fence, the path soon becomes impassable, and this is a good point to turn around and retrace your steps.

Walk 8
Grwyne Fawr Reservoir

There are two possible routes to the reservoir. The easy route follows the river upstream to where it emerges from the reservoir. Whilst the track is easy to follow, and offers pleasant views of the valley and the river, it does not allow the walker to see the true beauty of the Grwyne Fawr Reservoir as it only reaches the bottom of the reservoir. The extreme route climbs up the side of the valley and is constantly bumpy (although many little children enjoy this) and offers excellent views along the entire course of the walk. The views around the reservoir are delightful and it is a tranquil area. There are grassy areas alongside the banks of the water, where picnics and lazing about can

Distance	3.6 miles (5.9km) – easy route 4.1 miles (6.6km) – hard route
Ascent	495ft (151m) – easy route 706ft (215m) – hard route
Allow	Easy route – 2 hours; hard route – 3hours
Terrain	This walk takes ATPing to the extreme due to the rocky trail (note the word 'trail'!) which looks impossible for the first couple of hundred metres, although the ATP could be carried across this first section (or bumped at speed to the delight of many a toddler!) The path is never smooth and certainly not suitable for a young baby. The gradient is slow, and the path alternates between

Terrain (cont'd)	rough and smooth. Not for the faint hearted! Alternatively, the road leading up to the foot of the dam makes for a very easy walk. There is still some ascent, but the track is very pleasant to follow
Map	Explorer Map OL13 / Landranger Map 161. Grid ref SO 252 284
Amenities	Make sure you bring that potty! Plenty of mountain spring water along the route

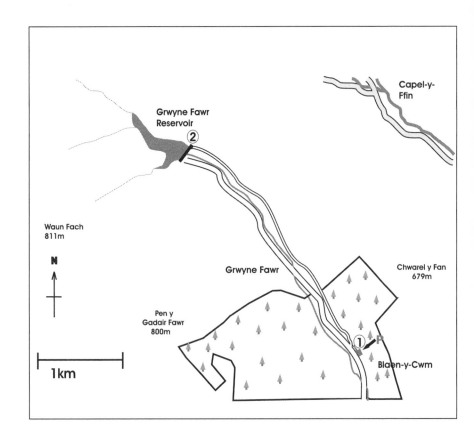

be enjoyed (although small children will inevitably do their best to prevent this!). There are a number of springs where children will enjoy tasting cold, fresh mountain water straight out of the rock on the walk. (Remember you should only drink spring water if you are confident of its source).

The track is rough and bumpy to some extent throughout

Directions to starting point

From the A465, turn into the village of Llanfihangel Crucorney sign posted Skirrid Inn, Llanthony Abbey (note that there are two turnings into the village). A short way down the road, take the turning which heads quite steeply downhill (signposted Llanthony). Pass under a bridge and follow the signs for Grwyne Fawr Reservoir. After a number of miles, there is a forestry commission car park on the right just over a small river. This is a delightful place to stop with a number of trails. Continue to the next car park, called Grwyne Fawr.

The Route

Extreme

Take the trail which starts from the far end of the car park. It soon joins the main trail (which is a bridleway). The main trail is incredibly rocky and quite difficult to negotiate for a couple of hundred metres. It improves somewhat after this, but is never smooth underfoot for long. You will soon pass through a gate.

1. Follow the trail until it reaches the reservoir. You are able to walk across the dam wall beneath the summit of Waun Fach (the highest mountain in the Black Mountains). You can also walk along the right hand side of the reservoir for a little distance, which has some pleasant places to sit. Retrace your steps back to the start.

Easy

2. Walk out of the car park to the road on which you have just been travelling, and walk in a north-westerly direction towards the reservoir. There is a gate to pass through and a bridge to cross. Follow the road/track until you can go no further, and then retrace your steps back to the car park.

The view up to the reservoir

Walk 9
Black Mountain

This is a very simple walk requiring very little, if any, map reading skills. The path is always obvious and is composed of smooth, grassy tracks. The gradient is steady, and increases a little towards the end. Although short, this walk shows a little of the wild, bleak aspect of the Black Mountain. Wildlife in the form of red kites, rabbits and wild ponies can often be seen. The imposing form of Carreg Cennen Castle is visible from the car park, and of course this walk could be combined with a visit to the romantic castle. (There is a circular walk around the castle, although it is not suitable for ATPs.) If eating a picnic, the car park is as good a place as any to eat, as here you may enjoy the fine views.

Distance	1.3 miles (2.1km)
Ascent	308ft (94m)
Allow	½ to 1 hour
Terrain	The path is easy going and smooth, and increases a little in steepness towards the end
Map	OS Explorer Map OL12 / Landranger Map 160. Grid ref SN 707 193
Amenities	The nearest toilets and shops are in Brynaman, although there are also a couple of shops in Llangadog although no toilets (except for in the pubs)

Directions to starting point

From Llangadog, take the A4069 towards Brynaman. Half way up climbing the mountain, take the turning right, just before a big hairpin bend. Drive just over a mile down the single track road, and you will come to a car park on your left. This is the starting point for the walk. If coming from the Brynaman side, as the road comes over the mountain and starts winding its way down the other side, take the left hand turning just after the hairpin bend (then follow the second part of the directions above).

The Route

1. From the car park, turn right (heading west towards Carreg Cennen Castle). In about 100 metres, take the obvious track on your left which is the start of the walk. After about 200 metres you will see

Looking down the track with Carreg Cennen Castle in the background

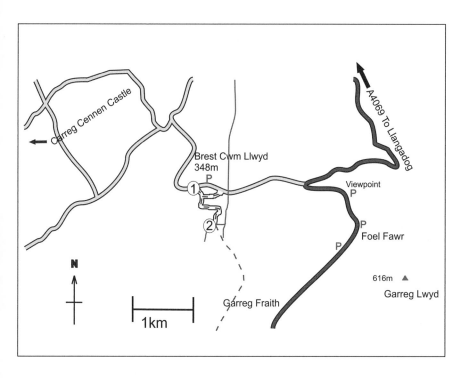

a track to your left which comes up from the road on which you have just travelled. Ignore this and continue. The track curves around the edge of the mountain spur and it starts to head up the valley. The path soon becomes steeper, and you will know when it comes to an end as it simply stops, and all that is ahead of you is the open hill. Very simply retrace your steps back to the car park.

Walk 10
Llyn y Fan Fach

Llyn y Fan Fach is a tranquil lake, steeped in legend and surrounded by the imposing ridge of Bannau Sir Gaer (the ridge leading to the highest point in the Black Mountain). It is a truly beautiful and remote location, giving a taste of the ruggedness of the Brecon Beacons. The track that leads to the lake is steep, but wide and even, involving strenuous uphill pushing. It follows a stream all the way to the lake,

Distance	**2.7 miles (4.4km)**
Ascent	**800ft (248m)**
Allow	**1½ - 2½ hours**
Terrain	**An excellent track that is very wide, and provides a constant uphill gradient and is quite a slog (as can be seen by the ascent). One narrow section where a double ATP will need to be carried for about 20 yards, although single ATPs will squeeze through**
Map	**OS Explorer Map OL12 / Landranger Map 160. Grid ref SN 799 238**
Amenities	**Public toilets in Sennybridge. Very useful and well stocked Londis Shop shortly after Sennybridge. Turning off the A40, take the signs for the Usk Reservoir, there is a park by the Antique Centre**

eventually passing the fisheries, where fish can be seen jumping much to the delight of young spectators! It involves one short section (of about 20 yards) where double ATPs need to be carried, although single ATPs will manage it.

Directions to starting point

From Brecon, take the A40 towards Llandovery. Take the first left in the village of Trecastle (next to the Castle Coaching Inn). Continue for 1.5 miles and take a left fork signposted Llanddeusant. Follow the road for another 6 miles (passing the turning for Usk Reservoir) until you reach the village of Talsarn. Take a sharp left turn and continue to follow the signs for Llyn y Fan. The road is narrow and eventually becomes a track shortly before reaching the parking area.

The Route

1. Follow the track that leaves the car parking area (not forgetting to read the information board recounting the legend of the Lady of the Lake).

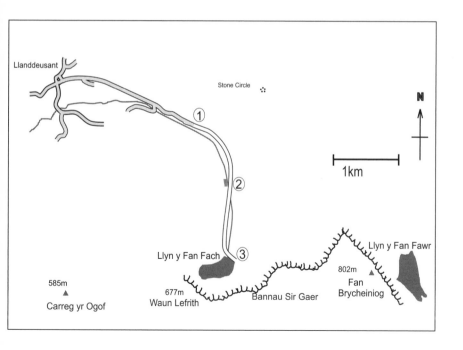

Llyn y Fan Fach provides the perfect picnic spot!

2. At the fisheries (half way there), there is a short section where double ATPs will need to be carried. Single ATPs will manage reasonably well.

3. The main path continues to the Lake. Descend via the same route.

Walk 11
Glyntawe Railway Track

This walk uses the old railway line that runs above the valley. It is a peaceful walk offering views across the valley towards the Carmarthen Fan (Bannau Sir Gaer), and the craggy hills around the Sleeping Giant (Cribarth). Although initially steep for short period, the track is broad, smooth and even. The annoying factor to note is that there are two gates over which the ATP will have to be lifted. If you also have children who are walking, it should also be noted that there are a few

Distance	3.9 miles (4.2km)
Ascent	406ft (124m)
Allow	1½ - 2½ hours
Terrain	Being a former railway line, the track is level and wide, with a short, steep start. It is muddy towards the end of the walk. There are a few gates to lift the ATP over
Map	OS Explorer Map OL12 / Landranger Map 160. Grid ref SN 867 192
Amenities	There are toilets 3 miles down the road at Craig-y-Nos Country Park (see Walk 22 for details on getting there). Toilets include baby changing (in the 24hr disabled toilet by the lake nearest to the car park), a vending machine and tea rooms. There is a village shop at Ynyswen a further two miles down the road towards Swansea

sections where the railway has been built up, and there is a considerable fall to either side.

NB Just before going to press, there has been a landslide that has temporarily stopped access to this walk. The path is going to be repaired, and there is a sign on the gate at the start of the walk giving advice on its current state.

Directions to starting point

From Brecon, take the A40 heading west, getting off onto the A4067 signposted Swansea at Sennybridge. Follow this road through the villages of Defynnog and Crai. Pass the Crai (Cray) Reservoir on your right. The road levels out as you pass the reservoir, and just as the road starts to fall, turn into the lay-by on the left hand side, which has a pair of gates, and stile with a track behind.

The excellent track although plagued by stiles, is a great walk with good views towards the Sleeping Giant above Craig-y-Nos

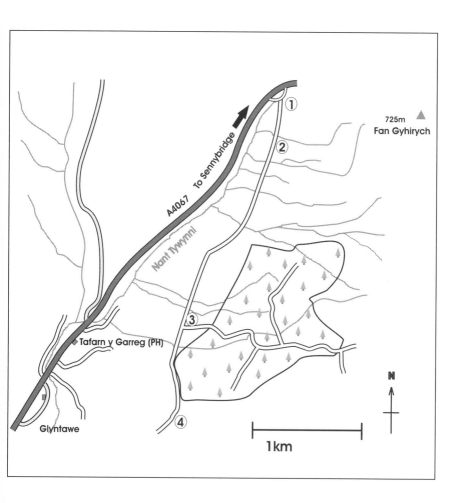

The Route

1. The gate is locked and the ATP will need to be lifted over it. The path is steep and a little rocky for the first fifty yards or so. Thereafter it levels out, and remains level for the duration of the walk. As the path levels out, it meets the old railway line which joins it from the left. Continue straight ahead.

2. After about a quarter of a mile, you will encounter a second locked gate again with a stile to the side of it just before a former railway

bridge. The ATP will probably need to be lifted over (although there are a series of gates alongside the track, and it may be possible to use them to avoid lifting the ATP). The path continues and for a short stretch, the railway line has been built up considerably, with a fall to the left hand side (note for any children who are walking). In another 300 yards or so, you will come across a third gate that is again locked and the ATP will need to be lifted over this one.

3. The track eventually leads abruptly to the left, heading into the forestry – don't take this. Continue straight ahead – the track is now grass covered, and more muddy.

4. When you eventually meet the fourth locked gate, unless you enjoy the experience of lifting ATPs over gates, now would be a good time to turn around (as the path quickly deteriorates past this final gate) and retrace your steps.

Walk 12
Fan Gyhirych

This walk gives the opportunity of getting close to the summit of an imposing mountain – Fan Gyhirych. Lovely views across to the Carmarthen Fan are to be enjoyed (weather permitting) for the whole of the walk, and then eventually across to Fan Nedd and to Pen y Fan in the distance. Although slightly rocky and a little steep initially, the track is fantastic – wide and with a fairly gentle gradient. It can be a little muddy during wet periods, although, in summer, dries up nicely. Little navigation is required as you stay on one track.

Distance	4.06 miles (6.53km)
Ascent	611ft (186m)
Allow	2-3 hours
Terrain	A fairly gradual, but continual climb on a wide and generally smooth, but sometimes muddy track. One gate to lift a double ATP over at the start of the walk (single ATPs should squeeze through)
Map	OS Explorer Map OL12 / Landranger Map 160. Grid ref SN 896 222
Amenities	There aren't any nearby. The closest toilets and food would be at Craig y Nos Country Park (5 ½ miles away, see Walk 22 for details), or the Mountain Centre at Libanus (6 ½ miles away, see Walk 15 for details)

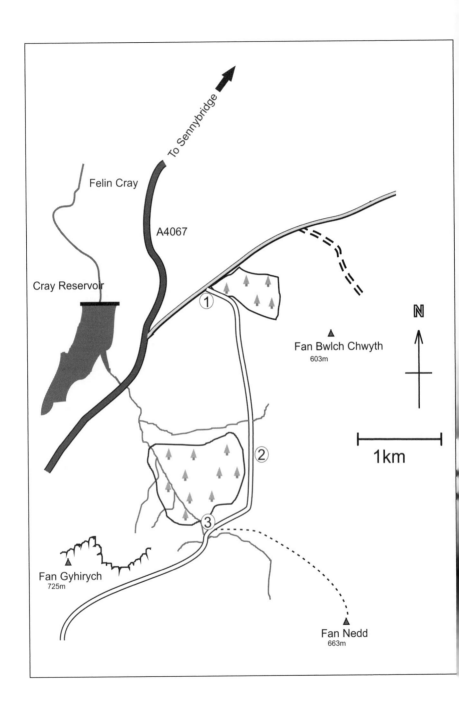

Directions to starting point

From Brecon, take the A40 heading west, getting off onto the A4067 (signposted Swansea) at Sennybridge. Follow this road through the villages of Defynnog and Crai, turning left by Crai (Cray) Reservoir, signposted Heol Senni. Follow this road for half a mile, and you will see a track on the right hand side heading up alongside the forestry. This is the start of the walk.

The Route

1. The gate is generally locked, and you may be able to negotiate your ATP around it or have to lift it over. The track, whilst a little stony to start with, is broad and climbs gently uphill. The track initially runs alongside forestry for a few hundred metres, then turns in a southerly direction, heading towards Fan Gyhirych.

An excellent path with the impressive sight of Fan Gyhirych in the background

2. After a mile, there is a track that leads off to the right into more forestry. Don't take this, stay on the main track for another ¾ of a mile.

3. You will see the remains of a stone wall ahead of you, and the path divides into two. Take the right fork. The left fork quickly turns into a footpath heading up Fan Nedd. The track continues for a short distance further until it comes to a locked gate and sheep pens. This makes a natural stopping point. The views are excellent and it can be a great picnic spot if not too windy. The return follows the same route back.

Looking across at the impressive sight of Fan Gyhirych

Walk 13
Fan Bwlch Chwyth

An interesting walk up to the former mine and quarry, with views towards the Llandovery countryside, and also across the Brecon Beacons Escarpments to Pen y Fan. There are a couple of buildings in which children will enjoy looking (which aren't dangerous), and you are able to walk on the flat area of the former quarry. The path although a little steep and rough to start with is generally very good, wide and stony underfoot. It is uphill to varying degrees for the outward leg.

Directions to starting point

From Brecon, take the A470 towards Merthyr Tydfil. A short distance after the sign post for Libanus (Mountain Centre), take the A4215. Follow this road for 2.3 miles, and take a left turning signposted Heol Senni and Ystradfellte. This is a narrow road and care is needed.

Distance	1.6 miles (2.6km)
Ascent	283ft (86m)
Allow	1 hour
Terrain	Steep and a little rough at the start, but generally good and wide
Map	OS Explorer Map OL12 / Landranger Map 160. Grid ref SN 907 228
Amenities	None. The nearest toilets and food are found at the Mountain Centre at Libanus (See Walk 15)

Follow the road which passes over a bridge at Heol Senni. It then begins to climb steeply and passes over a cattle grid. The road continues to climb. Immediately before the second cattle grid, there is a grassy area to the left where you can park the car.

The Route

1. Take the path ahead of you which is a little steep and rough (due to the track being eroded by water). The track continually bears to the right and swings around Fan Bwlch Chwyth. The stony track becomes a little wet in places (although not boggy) due to small, shallow streams flowing across it.

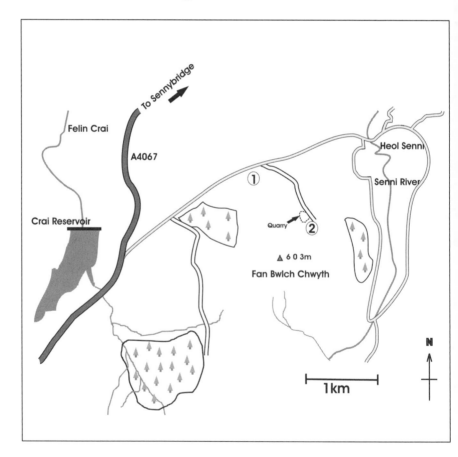

2. The track comes to a dead end, although walkers can continue, and this is where you need to turn around and retrace your steps. After turning around you will see a track that splits off to the left and climbs a short distance to the flat quarry. This is interesting to have a look at. Return via the same route.

The elevated track gives views across the Brecon Beacons escarpment and the surrounding countryside

Walk 14
Fan Frynych

This is an energetic walk (meaning the path is very steep) and a reasonable level of fitness and strength is required. It is probably advisable to walk it with someone else to take turns pushing! There is one gate over which the ATP must be lifted. Views across various sections of the Brecon Beacons make this a rewarding walk.

Directions to starting point
From Brecon, take the A470 towards Merthyr Tydfil. A short distance after the sign post for Libanus (Mountain Centre), take the A4215.

Distance	1.7 miles (2.7km)
Ascent	426ft (130m)
Allow	1½ - 2 hours
Terrain	The path is wide and straightforward, although for half of the walk it is very steep. A reasonable level of fitness and strength is required for this walk. If taking a double ATP, it would be advisable to walk it with someone else (to take turns pushing!). There is one locked gate to lift the ATP over after about ½ mile
Map	OS Explorer Map OL12 / Landranger Map 160. Grid ref SN 961 241
Amenities	There are toilets and a shop/café at the Mountain Centre, Libanus, which is 4 miles away (See Walk 15)

Take the left hand turning in just over a mile down a single track road. Follow this straight single track road for half a mile. When you reach a sharp right hand bend opposite the 'Forest Lodge Cottages', you have arrived. Park on the side of the road, away from the gateways.

The Route

1. Walk down the track, through a gate, and you will soon go over a cattle grid.

2. Immediately after the cattle grid, there is a track on the left which starts to head uphill.

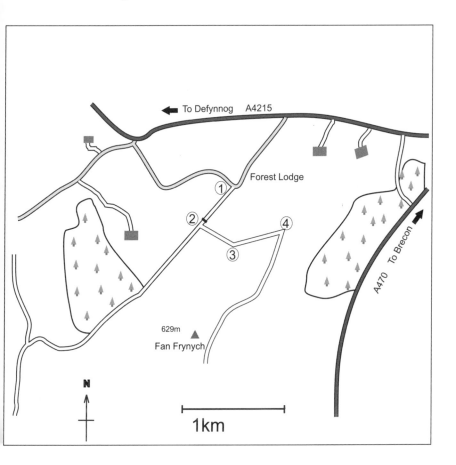

3. Go up the track and in three hundred yards, you will come to a locked gate with an information board about Craig Cerrig Gleisiad and Fan Frynych National Nature Reserve. You will have to lift your ATP over the gate.

4. The path is then very steep, and eventually levels out by a hairpin bend. You may now congratulate yourself on this arduous achievement and enjoy the views with which you have now been rewarded! Return via the same route. Extreme ATPers may be tempted to continue up the track from here, but this is not recommended as the steep descent would pose a risk to your children.

A constant steep pull gives some rewarding views

Walk 15
Mynydd Illtud, Libanus Mountain Centre

There are a number of paths across the common land surrounding the Mountain Centre which make this an excellent destination for a relaxing and enjoyable walk of any distance. The Mountain Centre provides good quality home cooked food (at reasonable prices), as well as the Brecon Beacons Visitor Centre, shop and toilets. The route is a circular walk. It is easy to make the walk into a gentle stroll if you don't fancy the final push up to the trig point. There are fantastic views of the Brecon Beacons with the panorama of Pen y Fan in the centre. The paths are excellent – smooth grass covered tracks.

Distance	2.7 miles (4.4km)
Ascent	264 ft (81m)
Allow	1½ - 2 hours
Terrain	Smooth, grassy tracks over the common which are generally well drained
Map	OS Explorer Map OL12 / Landranger Map 160. Grid ref SN 977 262
Amenities	There are toilets, a café (serving well priced, excellent home-cooked food) and shop at the Mountain Centre. There are maps, gifts, walking books and some walking equipment in the shop

Directions to starting point

From Brecon, take the A470 towards Merthyr Tydfil. In the village of Libanus, you will see a sign post on the right for the Brecon Beacons Visitor Centre. Follow this road until you see the Visitor Centre on the right. There is ample parking in the Centre. From the A4067, turn right in the village of Defynnog and follow the signs for the centre.

The Route

1. Starting in the car park with the Visitor Centre behind you, walk to end of the car park to the kissing gate. Fifty yards to your right is a gate which is more suitable for ATPs. If you go through that gate, go back to the beginning of the path at the kissing gate. You will see that the path divides into three. Take the right hand path which climbs slowly and runs parallel with the hedge. At the top of the bank there is a path that branches to the right. Ignore this and stay

Pen y Fan provides a beautiful backdrop for the length of the walk, on the excellent common paths

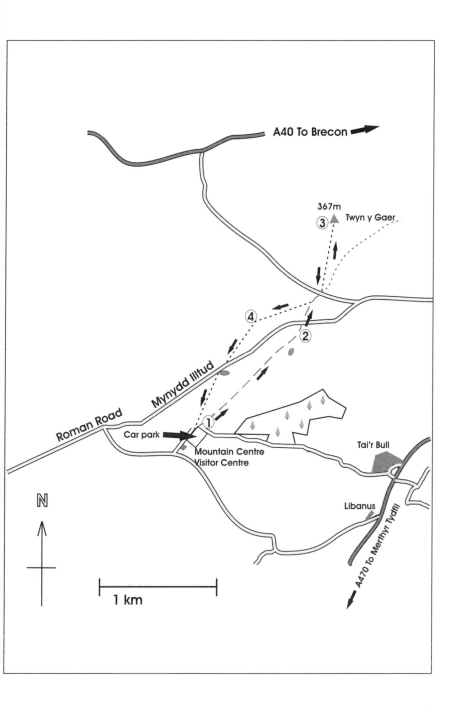

on the main track. You will be able to see a hill in the distance with a trig point on top which is your destination. One path breaks off sharply to the left – ignore it. In a short while the path forks. Take the left path which takes you almost immediately to the road.

2. You will see a bridleway sign which you follow quite steeply down to the next road. Cross the road and take the path which obviously leads straight up the hill to the trig point on top. It should be noted that the path is quite steep, and hard going depending on your fitness level and the weight of your loaded ATP. You may wish to pause under one of the mature oak trees for a picnic or respite.

3 Enjoy the views from the trig point! On the way back, after crossing the first road, take the path that cuts right following the edge of the field.

4. At the top of the hill after rounding the corner of the field, aim in a south-westerly direction (there are numerous tracks, and giving a multitude of directions here would not be particularly helpful). If you are unsure, head towards Fan Frynych (the escarpment to the right of Pen y Fan). As you have gained height you will soon see the visitor centre. Cross the road and head back to the car park which will be visible.

Walk 16
Tor Glas

Walk on the wild side. This is the most serious walk in the book. It climbs to 599 metres, very close to Fan y Big (719m), and not far from Pen y Fan (885m), and although the path is not too steep (and is driven by 4x4s during certain events), it is a constant slog, and the path is very stony. Weather in the Brecon Beacons changes quickly at times. It may be sunny at the bottom, but snowing on the summits. There will be a difference in temperature and the wind chill is a significant factor. A rain cover will provide excellent shelter for your child. If it

Distance	4.5 miles (7.2km)
Ascent	680ft (207m)
Allow	3-4 hours
Terrain	A very marked path, although difficult due to its stony nature. A constant incline
Map	OS Explorer Map OL12 / Landranger Map 160. Grid ref SO 035 174
Amenities	Don't forget the potty! There are toilets and a shop in Talybont. The toilets in Talybont are on the edge of the White Hart Inn. There is also a children's park in Talybont – go past the White Hart Inn with the canal on your left, take the next right (after the hump-backed bridge that goes over the canal) signposted recycling. Talybont has a great shop/post office which sells a bit of everything!

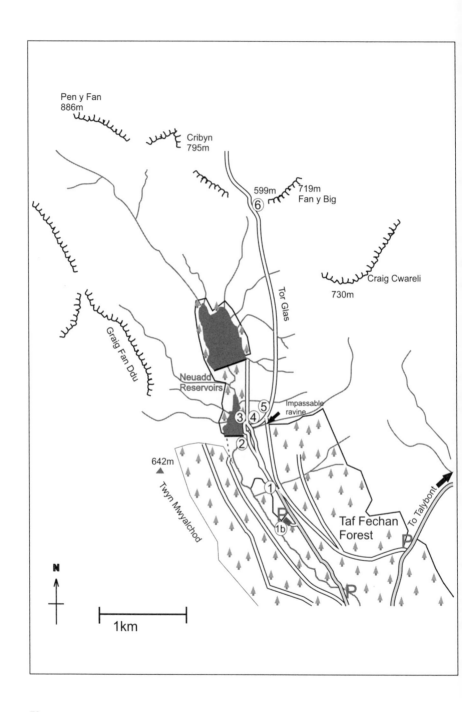

is a blisteringly hot day, remember there is no shelter over the course of the route. Just make sure you are prepared – hats, gloves, footmuff and waterproofs are sensible even in summer! You are really getting into the middle of the Brecon Beacons. In order to get a parking space, you will need to get there early, as there is only space for a couple of cars, and they go quickly. The views of Pen y Fan along the way are thoroughly rewarding.

Directions to starting point

From Brecon, take the A40 towards Abergavenny. After 4.5 miles, turn right signposted Talybont on Usk. Continue along Station Road to the T-junction and turn right. Pass the White Hart Inn, and the post office and take the next left, a hump-back bridge over the canal. Follow this road which drives alongside the reservoir, and then starts to climb as it heads into the forestry. On the top of the pass, you will drive over a cattle grid, drop back downhill a little way, over a narrow bridge, and then up to a junction. At the junction, turn right signposted Neuadd Reservoirs. Follow this road for just over a mile (being careful not to take an access road used by Welsh Water). You will reach a gate which says no vehicles beyond this point; Grid ref 035 174. This is the start of walk. Parking on the side of the road here is possible, although limited. If intending to do this walk, it is advisable to get here early. There is also a car park at Grid ref 037 170 (see (1b) in route directions), which adds about 1km extra to the walk.

The Route

1. Take the tarmac road (which says no vehicles beyond this point), not the track that starts off parallel with the tarmac road. (Although this might look inviting, it comes to an impassable ravine). In summertime, look out for dragon flies that fly up and down the little stream on the side of the road.

2. Just before the Lower Neuadd Reservoir, you will come to a gate. Go through it, around the water works buildings and up the short but steep road.

3. At the top of this road, take the track that doubles back behind the buildings.

A rough track takes you to the bottom of the Pen y Fan horseshoe

4. You will shortly come to a gate on the left hand side. Go through the gate and up the steep path for a short distance until you meet the main track.

5. Turn left so that you start climbing upwards towards the pass. This is quite a slog, and the path maintains an unrelenting incline. The path is rocky and a little tiresome!

6. When you eventually reach a gate, you are almost at the top of the pass. The pass is just beyond the gateway. Don't attempt to go down the other side, as it is steep, and suitable only for walkers and mountain bikers. You are now at 599m, with Fan y Big 500m east of you (719m), and Cribyn 1km north-west of you (795m). There are some sheltered spots if the wind has picked up. After some refreshments, although the path is still rocky, it is all downhill! Return via the same route.

1b. From the car park

If starting from the car park, turn left onto the road and follow it to the gate. Continue on the above route from no.1.

Walk 17
Neuadd Reservoirs

Pen y Fan is of course the highest mountain in the Brecon Beacons and the South of Britain at 886m. This is a really easy walk along good forrestry paths and tarmaced road that takes you past the two Neuadd Reservoirs and right to the bottom of the Pen y Fan horseshoe. Views to the surrounding mountains are terrific on a good day, and it makes for a relaxed, easy, enjoyable walk. It is possible to shorten the route by going to a closer car park if time is short.

Distance	4.1 miles (6.6km) 2.6 miles (4.1km) shorter route
Ascent	471ft (143m) / 209 ft (64m) shorter route
Allow	1½- 2½ hours /shorter route 1-1½ hours
Terrain	A combination of tarmac and easy tracks
Map	OS Explorer Map OL12 / Landranger Map 160. Grid ref SO 049 167 (or SO 037 170 if taking the slightly shorter route)
Amenities	Don't forget the potty! There are toilets and a shop in Talybont. The toilets in Talybont are on the edge of the White Hart Inn. There is also a children's park in Talybont – go past the White Hart Inn with the canal on your left, take the next right (after the hump bridge that goes over the canal) signposted recycling. Talybont has a great shop/post office which sells a bit of everything!

Excellent views across the Neuadd Reservoir to Pen y Fan

Directions to starting point

From Brecon, take theA40 towards Abergavenny. After 4.5 miles, turn right signposted Talybont on Usk. Continue along Station Road to the T-junction and turn right. Pass the White Hart Inn, and the post office and take the next left, a hump-back bridge over the canal. Follow this road which drives alongside Talybont Reservoir, and then starts to climb as it heads into the forestry. On the top of the pass, you will drive over a cattlegrid, and will then see a car parking area and track leading into the forestry on the right hand side.

Directions to shorter route starting point

If short of time, you may want to shorten the route. If so, drive past the car park, and in just under a mile, you will come to a junction. Turn right at the junction, and drive along the road for almost one mile – go over a bridge, and past a car park on the right hand side, until you come to the car park on the left hand side.

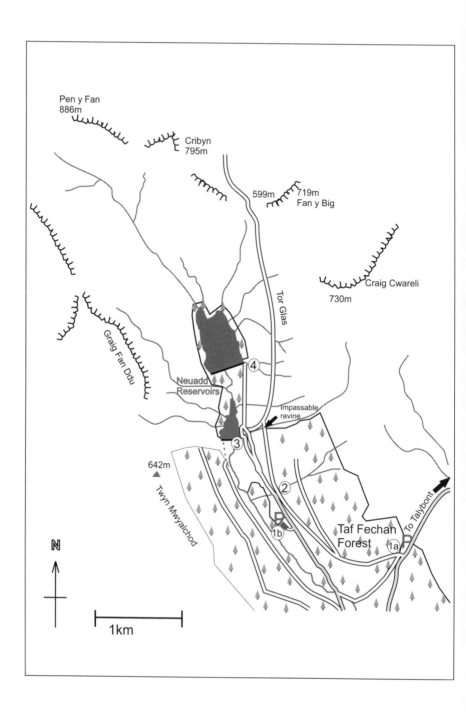

The Route

1a. From the parking area, take the Forestry Commission road that leads into the forestry by a green Forestry Commission gate (ATPs just fit under these gates!). Go over a little bridge which crosses a stream. 50 yards from the car park, veer right (not taking the track to your left). You will go through four gates, with the last gate located where the track joins the road.

2. Take the tarmac road (which says no vehicles beyond this point), not the track which starts off parallel with the tarmac road. (Although this might look inviting, it leads to an unpassable ravine.) Go through or around the big gate that is across the road and walk down the road (the ATP should fit under it, although you might have to tilt it back a little). In summer time, look out for dragon flies that fly up and down the little stream on the side of the road.

3. Just before the Lower Neuadd Reservoir, you will come to a gate. Go through it, around the water works buildings and up the short but steep road.

4. Follow this track to the Upper Neuadd Reservoir, enjoying the gorgeous views of Corn Du, Pen y Fan and the Cribyn horseshoe. Return via the same route.

Shorter Route

1b. If starting from the car park, turn left onto the road and follow the it to the gate. Continue on the above route from no. 2.

Walk 18
Blaen-y-Gwyn Waterfalls, Talybont

Although an short, easy walk, this is none the less worth doing for the tranquillity and views of the Blaen-y-Gwyn waterfalls. The path is quite difficult for the first 50 yards or so, but soon becomes much easier. There are a couple of fords to cross, so suitable footwear should be worn. Just for the sake of annoyance, there is a stile at the end of the

Distance	0.8 miles (1.34km)
Ascent	181ft (55m)
Allow	½ -1 hour
Terrain	The path is straightforward except for the first 50 yards. It is wide, and solid underfoot. There are a couple of fords to cross, and the ATP may have to be carried over the one ford. There is also a stile at the end of the walk which is necessary to cross if you wish to get closer to the waterfalls
Map	OS Explorer Map OL12 / Landranger Map 160. Grid ref SO 063 170
Amenities	The toilets in Talybont are on the edge of the White Hart Inn. There is also a children's park in Talybont. Going past the White Hart Inn with the canal on your left, take the next right (after the hump bridge that goes over the canal) signposted recycling

A short walk leads to an impressive waterfall

walk! An enjoyable picnic can be enjoyed on a grassy area not far from the waterfall.

Directions to starting point

From the A40, follow the signs for Talybont. In the village of Talybont, turn right at the junction. Pass the White Hart Inn, and the post office and take the next right, a hump-back bridge over the canal. Follow this road past the reservoir, over a small bridge, and you will see the car park on the right hand side.

The Route

1. In the car park, there is an information board giving some information about walks in the area. Take the track which leaves the end of the car park. It is stony and difficult to begin with, but soon becomes much more pleasant underfoot. There are two fords

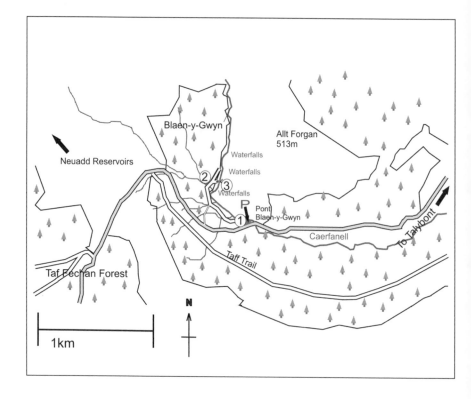

to cross, which are very shallow (although a little deeper after rainfall) and finally a small concrete bridge.

2. You will eventually come to the ruins of an old dwelling. Take the right fork which heads down to a stile.

3. Once over the stile, you have reached your destination. Return via the same route.

Walk 19
Talybont Reservoir – Taff Trail

The Talybont Reservoir is the largest reservoir in the Brecon Beacons. The walk skirts the reservoir and then follows part of the Taff trail for as little or as much as is required. There are views across the reservoir and the surrounding hills. The forestry commission path is smooth, wide and gently inclining on the way out and beautifully downhill on the way back! The trees give some protection from the elements.

Distance	**5 miles (8.2km)**
Ascent	**781ft (238m)**
Allow	**2-3 hours**
Terrain	**An excellent forestry commission track with a slow incline**
Map	**OS Explorer Map OL12 / Landranger Map 160/161 (most of the walk is covered by 161). Grid ref SO 103 205**
Amenities	**The toilets in Talybont are on the edge of the White Hart Inn. There is also a children's park in Talybont – go past the White Hart Inn with the canal on your left, take the next right (after the hump bridge that goes over the canal) signposted recycling. Talybont has a well stocked shop/post office!**

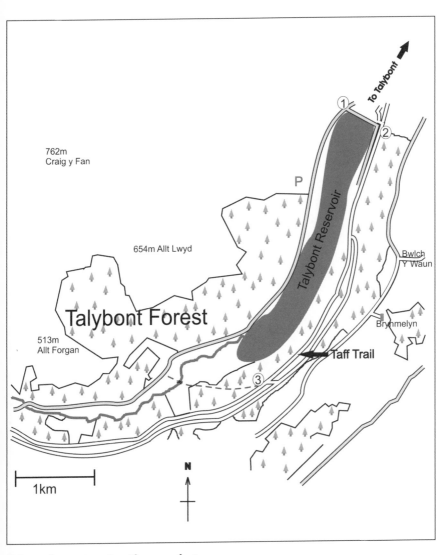

Directions to starting point

From the A40, follow the signs for Talybont. In the village of Talybont, turn right at the junction. Pass the White Hart Inn and the post office and take the next right, a hump-back bridge over the canal. Follow this road to the reservoir. There is space to park at the side of the reservoir.

The Route

1. Follow the road across the top of the dam wall.

2. On the other side of the wall take the track marked as the Taff Trail that heads along the side of the dam (don't take the narrow metalled road that runs immediately alongside the reservoir). Stay on the well marked trail for as long as you want returning via the same route.

3. Where a bridleway signposted Abercynafon cuts across the track, this is a good point to return (if you haven't already).

The Taff Trail track is well sheltered, and offers occasional views across Talybont Reservoir

Walk 20
Talybont Reservoir High Level Walk

One of the best and least known walks in the Brecon Beacons. The Talybont Reservoir is the largest reservoir in the Brecon Beacons. The walk runs at a height of about 400m above sea level, approximately 200m above the reservoir and offers stunning views across the reservoir, mountains and valley. The walk is very easy and

Distance	2.7 miles (4.5km), or if final section is walked: 4 miles (6.4km)
Ascent	316ft (96m), or if the final section is walked: 633ft (193m)
Allow	1-1½ hours / longer route 2 -2½ hours
Terrain	An excellent tarmac track until the final sections (4 and 5 on map). The final sections are fairly steep and rocky
Map	OS Explorer Map OL12 and 13 (most of the walk is on 13) / Landranger Map 161. Grid ref SO 110 187
Amenities	The toilets in Talybont are on the edge of the White Hart Inn. There is also a children's park in Talybont – go past the White Hart Inn with the canal on your left, take the next right (after the hump bridge that goes over the canal) signposted recycling. Talybont has a great shop/post office which sells a bit of everything!

straightforward, as it uses a slightly rough tarmac road. Because the route is at such a high level, it is very exposed to the elements, and this should be noted during colder weather. Your vehicle will have done all the climbing for you, and you can enjoy a fairly level route and the excellent views. On parking, there is a nice, grassy patch, ideal for picnicking. Decent boots are needed as there are two big muddy and wet sections later on in the walk.

Directions to starting point

From the A40, follow the signs for Talybont. In the village of Talybont, turn left at the junction (signposted Crickhowell and Llangynidr), and after 50 yards take the next right (signposted dead end). The road passes over the canal and is quite steep, climbing 320m in 2.5 miles. The road passes some forestry on the right, and then levels out by the turning for Bwlch yr Waun Farm, revealing lovely views across the Talybont Reservoir. There is space to park your vehicle here.

A lesser known high level trail above Talybont Reservoir with beautiful views through the Brecon Beacons

The Route

1. Follow the tarmac track that runs parallel with the reservoir.

2. As you drop down after the first rise, you will come to a gate just after the farm track that turns left for Brynmelyn. Ignore the track that comes out of the forestry joining the main track.

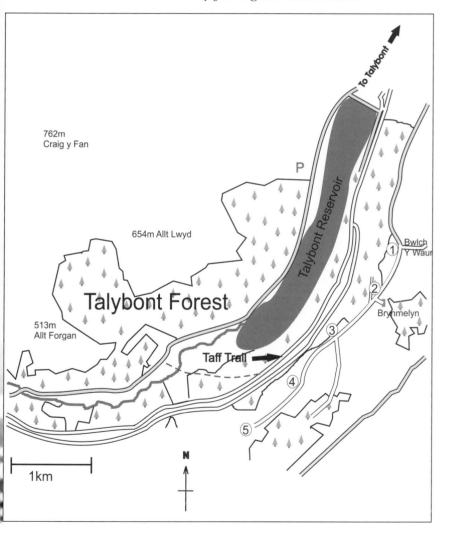

3. In a few hundred metres the track splits with one track going left, down into the forestry. You might enjoy the little stone bench here! The other track is sign posted Dolgaer – this is the track to take which is worn and stony. There are two big wet and muddy sections and is quite steep at times.

4. The track continues to another gate, and this may be a sensible place to turn around and retrace your steps.

5. If you are a hardened adventurer who enjoys pushing ATPs up difficult terrain, you could continue to the final gate. Beyond this, there is an impossible section for ATPs (incredibly steep with loose boulders).

Possibly the best view in the Brecon Beacons for the ATP walker

Walk 21
Sugar Loaf

This walk is an excellent introduction to walking with an ATP. The car has done most of the climbing, and you are able to enjoy broad, grassy tracks on the common. There are fine views to be enjoyed, as you are up at 1100 feet (330 metres). On a fine day, you will see the Sugar Loaf mountain ahead of you, and Blorenge mountain opposite you.

Directions to starting point
Heading from the direction of Brecon along the A40, pass through the town of Crickhowell, and then the village of Glangrwyney. After a

Distance	2.2 miles (3.5km)
Ascent	261ft (80m)
Allow	1- 1½ hours
Terrain	After an initial short, steep section at the start of the walk, the paths are easy and flat. The paths criss-cross the common land, and the grass is kept short by the sheep, so be prepared to clean the wheels of your ATP when you get home! (It may be useful to have a few carrier bags handy for putting the wheels into at the end of the walk)
Map	Explorer Map OL13 / Landranger Map 161 Grid ref SO 268 167
Amenities	There are toilets and shops in Crickhowell and Abergavenny

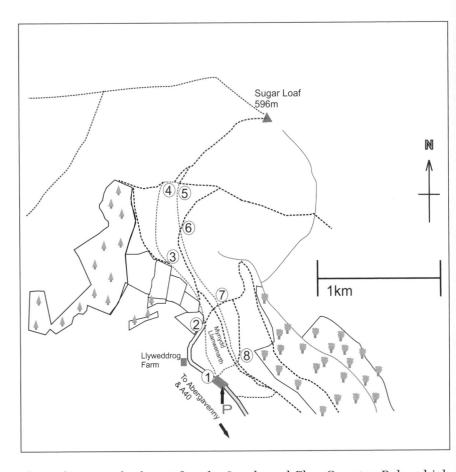

short distance, look out for the Lamb and Flag Country Pub, which has a crossroads signposted immediately after it. Turn left at the crossroads, which is also signposted for the Sugar Loaf Vineyards. (Please note these roads are extremely narrow and require care). Travel up the road for a hundred yards and turn left. Continue for another 100 yards and turn left at a junction, signposted Sugar Loaf and Sugar Loaf Vineyard. Continue along this road which worsens a little, go over a cattle grid and you will join a road (which has been built up) going to a farm on your right. Continue to head uphill, past one car park to the National Trust car park at the end of the road. You will notice a stone pillar view point showing the landmarks you can see around you.

The Route

1. From the car park, you will see three paths: a tarmac track leading from the car park and two paths leading up. Take the middle path – the path that leads to the left (the path to the right is steep – you will be coming down this at the end of the walk). The track is stony to start with and relatively steep, but soon becomes much smoother and gentler in gradient.

2. After 300 yards, you will come to the corner of a field with a stone wall where the track splits into two. Take the left track that follows the stone wall. Ignore the path that splits off to the right in a hundred yards. After another 200 yards, the path splits into two (you will also be able to see the edge of woods to your left), with the path on the left heading downhill. Ignore this, and ignore the two other paths that peel off towards the unmistakeable Sugar Loaf mountain.

3. Take the path that curves slowly to the right, aiming for the base of the Sugar Loaf. Eventually, this track makes an obvious split with the left hand track now going straight up the Sugar Loaf.

4. Take the right fork which joins the main track coming down from the Sugar Loaf.

5. Where the main track coming down from the Sugar Loaf meets the track you are on, take a 90 degree right turn onto the path descending the Sugar Loaf which heads for the ridge taking you back towards the start of the walk. Stay on this main track which now starts to head slightly downhill.

6. Ignore the track that heads right, stay on the main track which becomes quite worn.

7. At the top of the ridge, the path divides into three. Take the left path which starts to bear to the left.

8. You will come level with the start of some deciduous woodland to your left. A path cuts across the main track at 90 degrees. The track

The view across to Blorenge from the view finder

will soon head steeply down to the car park, and it is worth making sure you have your hand through the restraining loop of the cord attached to the ATP. You will pass a solitary tree shortly before reaching the car park.

Note

The directions may seen a little complicated, as there are a multitude of paths criss-crossing the common. Once you can see the Sugar Loaf mountain ahead of you, keep it behind you as you head away from it. Don't take the path that runs alongside the Sugar Loaf mountain, leading to the separate Rhoelben ridge that runs south-easterly. Stay on the more southly Mynydd Llanwenarth ridge, leading back to the car park.

Walk 22
Craig-y-Nos Country Park

Craig-y-Nos Country Park, currently managed by the Brecon Beacons National Park Authority is a 40-acre country park which forms part of the historic grounds of the Victorian Craig-y-Nos Castle. In addition to the walk described, the park has much to offer. There are numerous paths around the grounds, through trees (some of which make wonderful climbing frames!), alongside the river and lake, as well as stepping stones and a board walk. The walk described starts in the country park and leads up and along a path to the east of the park.

Distance	1.7 miles (2.8km)
Ascent	214ft (65m)
Allow	1 hour
Terrain	The track is generally wide, although there is one short, narrow section from the park to the bridleway. It is muddy at times due to horses using the track
Map	OS Explorer Map OL12 / Landranger Map 160. Grid ref SN 840 156
Amenities	Toilets include baby changing (in the 24hr disabled toilet by the lake nearest to the car park), vending machine and tea rooms. There is a shop at Ynyswen a further two miles down the road towards Swansea. Craig-y-Nos offer activities for children in the summer

The path that links the park to the bridleway is a little steep and narrow, although only 20 yards in length. The bridleway itself is muddy at times due to being used by horses.

Directions to starting point

From Brecon, take the A40 heading west, getting off onto the A4067 signposted Swansea at Sennybridge. Follow this road past Crai (Cray) Reservoir, until you reach the village of Glyntawe by Dan-yr-Ogof Caves. Just after the long straight, the road becomes twisty. Craig-y-Nos Country Park is on the left after the first couple of bends, immediately before the castle.

The Route

1. From the car park, walk towards the lake and follow the path as it goes away from the lake (past the disabled toilet) and runs alongside the river.

Lots of space for children to play in the Craig-y-Nos grounds

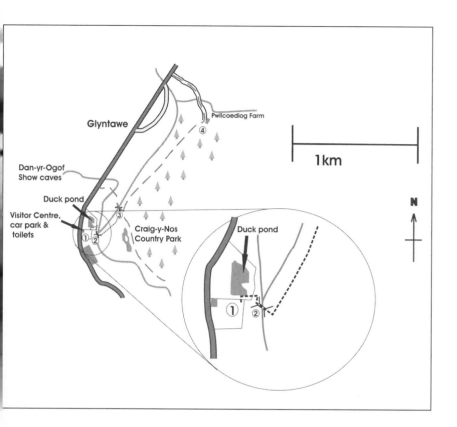

2. Cross the bridge and turn left following the river along the edge of the large grassy area. When you reach the stepping stones across the river (and the information board), you will see a fairly narrow and rocky path on your right heading upwards.

3. Go up the rocky path (which is awkward, and although seems impossibly narrow for double ATPs, it is passable and only 30 yards in length) until you reach the bridleway. Turn left on the bridleway.

4. In a few yards, there is a gate to go through. Follow the bridleway (being aware of the drop to start with on the left hand side) which has a few muddy patches due to horses, until you come to Pwllcoediog Farm and then retrace your steps back.

Walk 23
Penwyllt Tramway

The path follows a disused tramway, high up in the Brecon Beacons. It is real escapism, and feels quite remote and wild. It has some good views across the valley to towards the Carmarthen Fan (Bannau Sir Gaer). The main disappointment is the three gates over which your ATP needs to be lifted, although it is definitely worth the effort. The path is well drained, wide and dry. It has one short, steep, rocky

Distance	3 miles (4.9km)
Ascent	473ft (144m)
Allow	1½ - 2 hours
Terrain	The path is a disused tramway, and is therefore well drained, wide and dry, although there is a steep section near the start of the walk. There are three gates which need to be climbed on the route
Map	OS Explorer Map OL12 / Landranger Map 160. Grid ref SN 856 155
Amenities	There are toilets 1 mile down the road at Craig-y-Nos Country Park (see Walk 22 for details on getting there). Toilets include baby changing (which are open 24 hours per day), a vending machine and tea rooms. There is a shop at Ynyswen a further two miles down the road towards Swansea

A short, steep, rocky ascent leads to level paths in the tranquility of the Beacons

section, although after that has been negotiated, the path is flat and easy.

Directions to starting point

From Brecon, take the A40 heading west, getting off onto the A4067 signposted Swansea at Sennybridge. Follow this road through the villages of Defynnog, Crai (Cray), and eventually Craig-y-Nos. After passing through Craig-y-Nos, take the left hand turn signposted Penwyllt. The road crosses the river and takes a sharp left hand bend. Continue straight on, heading quite steeply uphill. Don't take the left turning at the start of the hill. The road eventually comes to what seems to be the entrance to a quarry. Follow the road over the cattle grid, which then turns right and after a hundred bumpy yards, opens out into a wide area, where you can park the car. The row of terraced houses you see is the South Wales Caving Club.

The Route

1. From the car parking area, walk to the kissing gate, and lift your ATP over it. After 50 yards another path joins the path you are on. Continue in the northerly direction. In another 100 yards or so there is a slightly faint path that branches off to the right. Stay on the main track which comes to a wide kissing gate. Lift your ATP over the gate and continue on the slightly bumpy tramway which after a short distance will join the main tramway.

2. Turn left onto the tramway which can be seen climbing into the distance. This is the steepest section. Although the section only lasts for a couple of hundred metres, it becomes increasingly steeper, and rocky towards the top. Once at the top of the visible cutting, the hard work has been done! It then flattens out and ahead is a strange ruined building and beyond, a stone wall with a

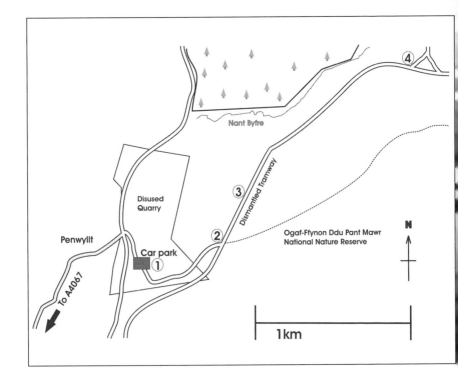

gate. There is a sign telling you about the Ogof Ffynnnon Ddu National Nature Reserve.

3. The gate is locked and this last hassle is worth the effort as the views up the valley are beautiful. Lift your ATP over the gate, and continue on the track as it follows a slow bend and heads north-east into the wilderness, passing two disused quarries. It deteriorates a little for a short distance and a small stream is crossed. The track follows the edge of the forestry, making a slow curve to the east and joining up with a more major track from the forestry. This is a good point to turn around.

Walk 24
Sarn Helen – Roman Road, Ystradfellte

This is a fantastic walk which takes in a variety of scenery, from the Nedd Fechan River, to woodland, to views across the Beacons. The walk offers some of the tranquillity and wildness of the Brecon Beacons. The track is generally good, although can be a little muddy in parts.

Directions to starting point
From Brecon the most straight forward route is to take the A470 out of Brecon, heading towards Merthyr Tydfil. Just after Libanus, take the A4215 and, after 2 miles, take the Heol Senni road. Take the fourth turning left in 1.5 miles, sign posted Ystradfellte. At the T-junction in just under two miles go left (which is almost straight on). The road soon climbs very steeply with a number of hairpin bends and then

Distance	2 miles (3.2km)
Ascent	348ft (106m)
Allow	1½ -2 hours
Terrain	Well defined tracks, a little bumpy in places, but generally good. Can be muddy in parts
Map	OS Explorer Map OL12 / Landranger Map 160. Grid ref SN 912 140
Amenities	There are toilets at SN 928 124. There is also a post office in the village and a very useful little shop/garage about a 2 miles south of the village (on the road to Pontneddfechan)

Fine views towards the quietness of Fan Nedd

starts to drop down into Ystradfellte. Drive through the centre of the village heading towards Pontneddfechan. After 1.3 miles, take the road sign posted Nedd Valley. Drive down this road, past the pretty white farm house with a pond at the front, and pull off the road, immediately past the turning left (which is steep). This is the start of the walk.

The Route

1. Walk down the track which descends sharply, then crosses the river and bears sharp left. Ignore the farm track that branches off to the right (saying No. 1). Continue on the slightly bumpy track which now goes through a small wooded section, and go through the gate.

2. The track leaves the wooded section and meets the Sarn Helen Roman road. Turn right and go through a metal gate. Take the track

that bears to the right around the forestry (not the track that goes straight into the forestry).

3. The path then divides again in a few hundred yards. Ignore the path to the right which is sign posted Sarn Helen and leads downhill (to

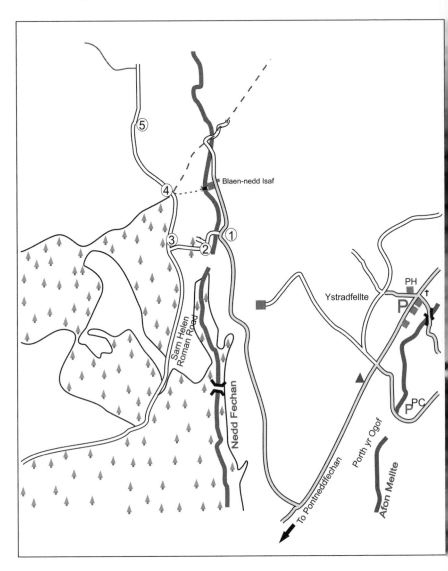

the Nedd Fechan River). Continue on the broad track which is now signposted Penwyllt. You will come to a locked gate, but with a little careful manoeuvring you should be able to get through the two gates to the side (used for sheep). After a few hundred yards there is a track heading off to the left, signposted Penwyllt. Don't take this (it soon deteriorates into an unsuitable footpath), again stay on the broader track.

4. In a short while you will reach a rocky area; this is an ideal spot to enjoy the tranquillity and wilderness of the Brecon Beacons, with views of Fan Nedd, and towards the back of Fan Gyhirich. Return via the same route.

This track will eventually (after a couple of miles) lead to Penwyllt, or Fan Gyhirich.

Walk 25
Carnau Gwynion, Ystradfellte

This is a lovely walk that takes you onto the rocky outcrops above the village of Ystradfellte (a beautiful, quaint, tiny village that won 'Powys Village of the Year' in 2004). It gives fantastic views around the

Distance	3.17 miles (5.21km)
Ascent	481ft (146m)
Allow	2 - 2½ hours
Terrain	The path is generally very good. There is one section which is a little awkward as vehicles have made the tracks deep, although it is possible to go around some of them. Also the track becomes steeper as it drops down into Ystradfellte. It is best not to reverse this route if using a double ATP for this reason
Map	OS Explorer Map OL12 / Landranger Map 160. Grid ref SN 926 154
Amenities	There are toilets at SN 928 124, and there is a car park in the middle of Ystradfellte at the start of the walk. There is also a post office in the village and a very useful little shop/garage about a 2 miles south of the village (on the road to Pontneddfechan). The New Inn Pub (in the middle of Ystradfellte) has a good reputation for food (at the time of writing!)

Beacons including Pen y Fan. You achieve what feels like remoteness even though you are never far from the village. There is lovely scenery accented by stone walls and limestone kilns, in addition to geological features – sink holes. These are formed where underground limestone caverns have dissolved and collapsed and formed what look like shell holes, and often become small pools. The track is generally good, although vehicles have created ruts in one section, although these are passable.

Directions to start of walk

From Brecon the most straight forward route is to take the A470 out of Brecon, heading towards Merthyr Tydfil. Just after Libanus, take the A4215 and after 2 miles, take the Heol Senni road. Take the fourth turning left in 1.5 miles sign posted Ystradfellte. At the T-junction in just under two miles take the left turn (which is almost straight on). The road soon climbs very steeply with a number of hairpin bends and then starts to drop down into Ystradfellte. In the centre of the small village, there is a car park where four roads meet. The walk starts from here.

The Route

1. From the car park, walk to the centre of the crossroads, and leave the village, heading north (with the New Inn Pub on your left). The road climbs a little and goes through the middle of a farm. As it leaves the farm, it becomes steeper. You will have gained 100m of the total 146m ascent – which might make you feel better! Nearly a mile from the farm, you will see a stony track on the left. Grid ref 926 154.

2. Turn left onto the stony track. After a couple of hundred metres you will come to a gate. Go through the gate bearing sharp right. The track is now grassy with stone walls on both sides. You will come to another gate in another couple of hundred metres.

3. Go through the gate and take the path that heads towards the rocky outcrop. You will see the remains of a limestone kiln which little ones will probably enjoy exploring! The track now goes downhill between rocky outcrops, and you will notice 'sink holes' on either

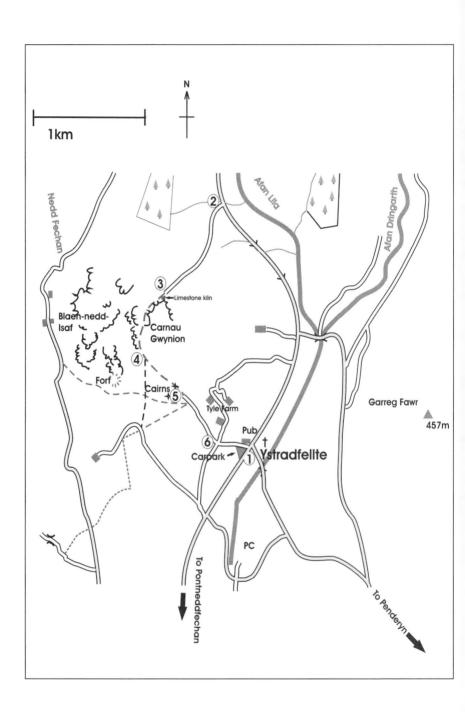

side of the path, a couple having filled with water. As you leave the outcrop you go through another gate.

4. The track becomes a little tricky now as the vehicle ruts become deep. The track leads to another gate, with a sign post next to it.

5. Go through the gate and continue on the track which now has a fence either side of it. The track leads to another gate. Go through the gate and continue along the track. The track becomes a little rocky and a little steeper.

6. The track then comes to a cross roads. Go straight across it and you will soon be back onto a tarmac road that leads to the car park and the centre of the village.

(Don't be put off by the last few detailed directions – you can't really go wrong).

An interesting path above the village of Ystrafellte

Walk 26
Wern Walk – Garw Nant Visitor Centre

The visitor centre can make for a full and fun packed day, with various activities on offer. There are mountain bike trails for beginners (children) including a beginners' mountain bike park. Children will enjoy the sculptured animal trail which is always popular with younger children, and a short nature trail – which can be combined as they are fairly short in length. There are also orienteering routes of varying ability. In addition there is an excellent children's play area (older and younger separated), as well as a good café, and a shop. An

Distance	2 miles (4.4km)
Ascent	800ft (103m)
Allow	1 - 1½ hours
Terrain	An easy walk with generally good forestry tracks. It is a little muddy at times, and there are two small streams to cross. Well sheltered with some pleasant views
Map	OS Explorer Map OL12 / Landranger Map 160. Grid ref SN 003 131
Amenities	Toilets, new café, children's play areas (under 7's, over 7's), mountain bike trails, picnic tables, gift shop, a few walks from which to choose. Free parking

A straight forward walk at the forestry centre which has much to offer

excellent day out for the all the family. The Wern Walk is a gentle, sheltered walk along well defined forestry tracks with pleasant views.

Directions to starting point

Garw Nant is situated just off the A470, 4 miles north of Merthyr Tydfil, between the Cantref and Llwyn-on Reservoirs. If travelling from Brecon, it is five miles after Storey Arms (again, between the reservoirs). It is well sign posted from the A470.

The Route

Follow the signs for the Wern walk which is clearly marked. From the visitor centre, head north past the adventure playgrounds. The path starts first on tarmac, then forestry tracks, and then slightly boggy grass before reaching a forestry track again. There are two small streams to cross. It is a little steep in a few parts, although quite

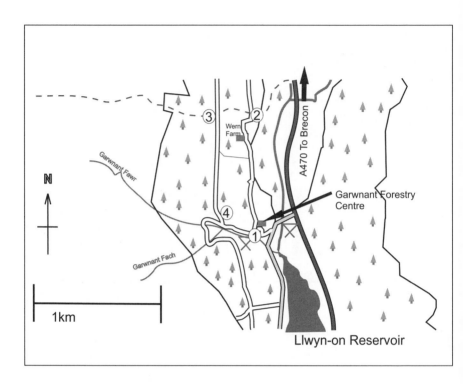

walkable with both single and double ATPs. It is a pleasant, sheltered walk on the whole. Pleasant views can be enjoyed at certain intervals along the walk. The walk passes by the ruins of Wern Farm.

Walk 27
Pontsarn Viaduct Taff Trail/ Pontsticill Reservoir

This is an easy walk following the Taff Trail, with a gentle ascent (although the total height gained is quite impressive) which follows the course of the old Brecon-Merthyr railway line, and goes over the viaduct. The path is tarmaced and the walk is covered in trees which although pleasant, limit the view at times. If so desired, the walk could be lengthened by continuing along the road to the nearby village of Pontsticill and the reservoir.

Distance	**2.8 miles (4.5km) or 4.3 miles (7km) (if you extend the walk to the reservoir)**
Ascent	**730ft (223m) or 907ft (277m) (if you extend the walk to the reservoir)**
Allow	**1 - 1½ hours** **Extended route: 2 - 2½ hours**
Terrain	**Easy tarmac paths**
Map	**OS Explorer Map OL12 / Landranger Map 160. Grid ref SO 044 098**
Amenities	**There are toilets in the nearby village of Pontsticill, although the nearest shops are in the village of Vaynor**

Directions to starting point

From Brecon, take the A470 until you reach the roundabout where it meets the A465 (the heads of the valley road) just outside Merthyr Tydfil. Take the first exit which is the A465 (heading towards Abergavenny), and then take the first exit off the A465 which is in about 150 yards, signposted Cefn Coed y Cymmer and Prince Charles Hospital. Follow this road for a couple of hundred yards to a crossroads. Go straight over the crossroads, and you will soon travel through the village of Trefechan (which is part of Merthyr Tydfil). Shortly after leaving the village, you will see the quarry on your left. The road then bends very sharply and passes underneath a wooden footbridge (that is part of the Taff Trail). After the turning right for Dowlais (sign mentions a width restriction), you will see a car park on the left hand side with an orange barrier (immediately before the road passes over a hump back bridge) - this is the starting point. At the

The impressive viaduct at Pontsarn

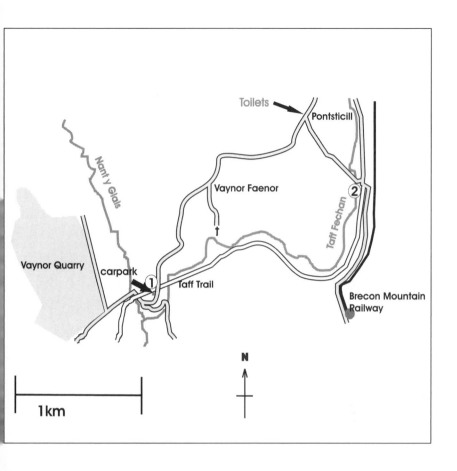

time of writing, the car park is not being used, although there is ample parking on the side of the road. The walk starts from the car park.

The Route

1. In the car park, you will see an information board, which gives some interesting information on the surrounding area including walks and history. Take the path which is just a few yards away leading to the Taff Trail. Turn right at the Taff Trail (if you went in the opposite direction, you pass over the wooden bridge that you drove under and head back to Trefechan).

2. Be aware that the Taff Trail follows the course of the Taf Fechan river (to your left), and there is some exposure to it at a couple of points. Follow the Taff trail which passes through two gates (both will take a double ATP after finding the correct gate to open!), and winds slowly up the valley until you reach the road. At this point you need to decide if you wish to turn around, or follow the road north (left as you reach it) to the reservoir and village of Pontsticill. Returning is a reversal of the route.

A gradual ascent on tarmac makes for an easy walk

Walk 28
Blorenge

This is a lovely little walk that offers an excellent path, and excellent views across the Black Mountains. It is easy to get to from Abergavenny and the surrounding area, making it a walk that can be fitted in without quite so much planning as others. No navigational skills are needed.

Directions to starting point

From Brecon, take the A40 to Abergavenny. Go into the town, and take the A4143 signposted A465 and Llanfoist. Drive through Llanfoist on the B4246, go under the bridge, and take a left heading for Brynmawr /Big Pit (weight restrictions on road). Go over a cattle grid, and just after a lay-by on the left, there is a second smaller one on the left, with

Distance	1.7 miles (2.8km)
Ascent	92ft (28m)
Allow	1 hour
Terrain	Excellent grassy track, very easy walking. No incline!
Map	OS Explorer Map OL12 / Landranger Map 160. Grid ref SO 259 121
Amenities	There is a Waitrose Supermarket in Llanfoist, which is very convenient for food and toilets, which has quick access from the A465

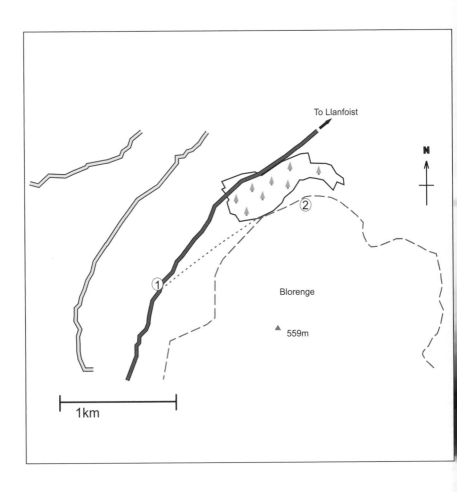

a footpath signpost showing Llanfoist/Garnddyrys. This is the start of the walk.

The Route

1. From the lay-by, walk along the track in the direction of Llanfoist. After a hundred yards, there are some gorse bushes which encroach on the path and it is a little bit narrow if you are using a double ATP, although manageable. Follow the path as you eventually walk past the forestry.

2. You come to a natural end when the path suddenly becomes very narrow, steep and impassable. Turn around and follow the track back.

The view towards the Black Mountains from the lower parts of Blorenge

Walk 29
Llanfoist Canal

This circular walk uses the Llanfoist-Gofilon Line (L-G Line) for a short distance before connecting to the Brecon-Usk Canal, and enjoying its tranquillity for half of the walk. It then links to a minor road, which heads steeply down to the B4269 and follows it for 300 metres before cutting back into the village of Llanfoist and back to the starting point. There are often ducks to be seen on the waterway, as well as many other forms of wildlife. There are also some good views across the Black Mountains, although the canal has a tree canopy over it, offering some shelter from the elements and obstructing views!

Distance	2.9 miles (4.6km)
Ascent	312 feet (95m)
Allow	1 - 1½ hours
Terrain	The first part of the walk uses the L-G Line former railway line which is very gently sloping and tarmaced. The path that links the L-G Line to the canal is quite steep, but only 100 yards in length. The canal path is flat and wide. A tarmaced road finishes the walk
Map	OS Explorer Map OL13 / Landranger Map 161. Grid ref SO 285 133
Amenities	There is a Waitrose Supermarket in Llanfoist, which has quick access from the main road

The canal offers a lovely circular walk

Directions to starting point

From Brecon, take the A40 to Abergavenny. Go into the town, and take the A4143 signposted A465 and Llanfoist. Drive into Llanfoist, staying on the main road. You will pass the post office on the left and notice speed bumps on the road. As you start to leave the village, there are more speed bumps and the road narrows (speed restrictions). Turn immediately right before the road narrows, signposted the village hall and car park. The car park is the starting point of the walk.

The Route

1. From the car park, go through the gate at the start of the Llanfoist Gofilon Line. You will pass over two bridges, the second one with a little bench.

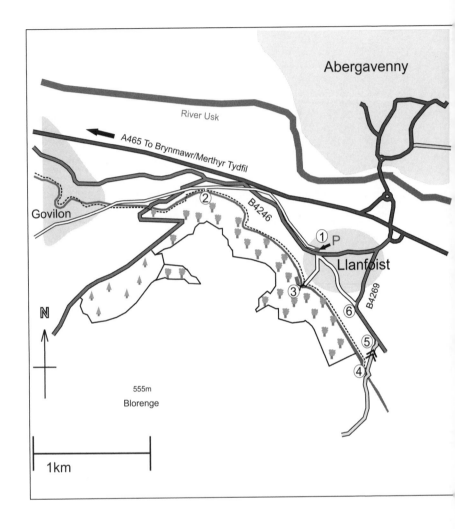

2. Take the path on the left that zig zags up quite steeply to the cana above and turn left. Follow the path down the side of the canal.

3. Pass under a bridge, and continue along the canal bank.

4. You will eventually reach another bridge. Go through a gate on the left just before the bridge and turn left onto the road which head downhill steeply.

5. There are some good views of Skirrid mountain ahead of you. The road meets the main road (B4269). Turn left onto the road. You will soon see a right hand bend ahead of you. Cross the road before it, as the bend is blind.

6. Take the first left hand turn that you see, which goes into the village. Stay on the road, through the no entry signs, past the school and church until the road reaches the main road and the car park where you started from is opposite.

Walk 30
Sgwyd Gwladus Waterfalls, Pontneddfechan

Known as 'Waterfall Country' as the area is teeming with them, this is a very tranquil and scenic walk that takes you to Sgwyd Gwladus (Gladys' Waterfall). The path takes you through a beautiful deciduous woodland canopy, following the course of the river. There is a picnic spot and opportunity to see bird life, as well as interesting caves along the way. For double ATPs, it is most sensible to turn around at the picnic site, as there are two difficult stepped sections, as well as a narrow section of path. Plenty of views are seen up to this point and it is still worthwhile, particularly as you reach the picnic area. Single ATPs can reach the waterfall with care and some carrying of the ATP.

Distance	2.3 miles (3.7km)
Ascent	390ft (119m)
Allow	1 - 1½ hours
Terrain	For two thirds of the walk, the path is very good – fairly flat, broad and easy. It does become more awkward with steps, tree roots and a narrow section before reaching the waterfall which necessitates some carrying of the ATP
Map	OS Explorer Map OL12 / Landranger Map 160. Grid ref SN 900 076
Amenities	There are toilets in the car park, and shops and fuel in Glynneath, just down the road. Food is served in the Angel Inn